CONCORDIA UNIVERSITY
DS489.5.F3
CEYLON LONDON

YO-CLJ-962

3 4211 000025225

CEYLON
A Divided Nation

The Institute of Race Relations is an unofficial and non-political body, founded in 1958 to encourage and facilitate the study of the relations between races. The Institute is precluded by the Memorandum and Articles of its incorporation from expressing an opinion on any aspect of the relations between races. Any opinions expressed in this work are therefore not those of the Institute.

CEYLON
A Divided Nation

B. H. FARMER

With a Foreword by
The Right Honourable The Viscount Soulbury,
G.C.M.G., G.C.V.O., O.B.E., M.C.

*Issued under the auspices of the
Institute of Race Relations*

OXFORD UNIVERSITY PRESS

LONDON   NEW YORK   BOMBAY

1963

Oxford University Press, Amen House, London E.C.4

GLASGOW NEW YORK TORONTO MELBOURNE WELLINGTON
BOMBAY CALCUTTA MADRAS KARACHI LAHORE DACCA
CAPE TOWN SALISBURY NAIROBI IBADAN ACCRA
KUALA LUMPUR HONG KONG

© Institute of Race Relations 1963

Printed in Great Britain by R. J. Acford Ltd., Chichester

CONTENTS

		PAGE
	FOREWORD *by* THE RIGHT HONOURABLE THE VISCOUNT SOULBURY, G.C.M.G., G.C.V.O., O.B.E., M.C.	vii
	INTRODUCTION	xi
I.	THE LAND OF CEYLON AND ITS PEOPLING: FACT, MYTH AND CONFLICT	1
II.	FOUR HUNDRED AND FIFTY YEARS OF FOREIGN RULE: THE PORTUGUESE AND THE DUTCH	16
III.	FOUR HUNDRED AND FIFTY YEARS OF FOREIGN RULE: THE BRITISH IN CEYLON	33
IV.	CEYLON SINCE INDEPENDENCE	59
	SELECT BIBLIOGRAPHY	73

MAPS

Map 1 Ceylon: relief, climatic divisions and towns .. xiv

Map 2 Ceylon: size and communal composition of District population according to the 1953 census. 60

FOREWORD

In promoting the advance to self-government and independence of the various communities comprised within the British Commonwealth and Empire, the relations of minorities to majorities have constituted one of the most contentious and complicated problems confronting successive British Governments. Mr. Farmer's brilliant exposition of this problem, as it has affected Ceylon, provides a striking example of its complexity.

A Commission, of which I had the honour to be the Chairman, was appointed by the British Government in 1944, to examine and discuss proposals for the constitutional reform of Ceylon. It did not take long to discover that the relations of minorities to majorities, and particularly of the Tamil minority in the northern and eastern provinces to the Sinhalese majority further south, were in the words of the Commission's report 'the most difficult of the many problems involved'. The Commission had of course a cursory knowledge of the age-long antagonism between these two communities, but might have been less hopeful of a solution had Mr. Farmer's book been available to underline the deplorable effect of centuries of troubled history upon the Ceylonese of today. The Commission devoted a substantial portion of its report to this minority question, and stated that it was satisfied that the Government of Ceylon was fully aware that the contentment of the minorities was essential not only to their own well-being but to the well-being of the island as a whole. And to quote the Commission's report: 'If it were otherwise, no safeguard that we could devise would in the long run be of much avail.' Recent years have shown that this observation was only too true.

But had Mr. D. S. Senanayake, the first Prime Minister of independent Ceylon, lived I cannot believe that the shocking events of 1958 and the grave tension that now exists between Tamils and Sinhalese would ever have occurred. Mr. Senanayake would have scorned the spurious electoral advantages that a less far-sighted Sinhalese politician might expect to reap from exploiting the religious, linguistic and cultural differences between the two communities, for it was his policy to make Ceylon a united nation and, as he told the State Council in November 1945 in his great speech recommending the proposals of the British Government, 'The Tamils are essential to the welfare of this island'.

Unhappily and for reasons indicated by Mr. Farmer, the death of Mr. D. S. Senanayake led to the eventual adoption of a different policy which he would never have countenanced. Needless to say the consequences have been a bitter disappointment to myself and my fellow Commissioners. While the Commission was in Ceylon, the speeches of certain Sinhalese politicians calling for the solidarity of the Sinhalese and threatening the suppression of the Tamils emphasised the need for constitutional safeguards on behalf of that and other minorities, despite the confidence felt by the Commission in Mr. D. S. Senanayake and any Government under his control. As Sir Charles Jeffries has put it in his admirable book, *Ceylon—The Path to Independence*, 'The Soulbury constitution . . . had entrenched in it all the protective provisions for minorities that the wit of man could devise'. Nevertheless—in the light of later happenings—I now think it is a pity that the Commission did not also recommend the entrenchment in the constitution of guarantees of fundamental rights, on the lines enacted in the constitutions of India, Pakistan, Malaya, Nigeria and elsewhere.

Perhaps in any subsequent amendment of Ceylon's constitution those in authority might take note of the proclamation made by the delegates at the African conference which met in Lagos two years ago: 'Fundamental human rights, especially the right to individual liberty, should be written and entrenched in the constitutions of all countries'. Nevertheless the reconciliation of Tamils and

FOREWORD

Sinhalese will depend not on constitutional guarantees but on the goodwill, common sense and humanity of the Government in power and the people who elect it.

If, as I hope, Mr. Farmer's book will influence public opinion in that direction, he will have made a notable contribution to the peace and prosperity of Ceylon.

SOULBURY.

INTRODUCTION

> We belong to one nation ... Differences in language do not prevent us from being a nation ...
> I.D.S. and M.I. WEERAWARDENA[1]

> What are we left with? A nation in ruins, some grim lessons which we cannot afford to forget and a momentous question: Have the Sinhalese and Tamils reached the parting of the ways?
> TARZIE VITTACHI[2]

WHEN Mr. Philip Mason, the Director of the Institute of Race Relations, first wrote to me about the possibility of producing a booklet about Ceylon he told me of a film unit that proposed round about 1948 to produce a documentary about that exquisite island and, seeking for a title, could find nothing more dramatic or sensational than *Ceylon: Island without Problems*. That could not possibly be the title of this booklet, for Ceylon in 1963, fifteen years after the coming of independence, abounds with problems, not least that of the relations between the Sinhalese majority and the Tamil minorities.

Or, to put the matter another way round, Ceylon was, for some years after it became independent on 4 February 1948, held up as a model for all the world of the way in which a colony might peacefully and by easy stages attain full independence without suffering those communal tensions that severed Pakistan from the Republic of India. Then, unheralded by premonitory rumbles felt in the outside world, there came in 1956 a period in which politics suddenly took on an air of instability; in which Cabinet dissension, the assassination of the Prime Minister (Mr. S. W. R. D. Bandaranaike) and states of emergency followed each other in quick succession; and in which communal disharmony led to a series of riots and to the particularly disgraceful clashes of 1958.

[1] I.D.S. and M. I. Weerawardena, *Ceylon and Her Citizens* (Madras, etc., Oxford University Press, 1956), p. 15.
[2] Tarzie Vittachi, *Emergency '58* (London, André Deutsch, 1958), p. 117.

What had happened to the apparently peaceful, well-governed and harmonious inter-community life of 1948? Was the harmony of 1948 more apparent than real? Have communal tensions a long history, or are they the product of new forces that have emerged in recent years? It is the object of this short booklet to seek the answer to these questions. It will begin to do so by sketching the main features of the island in which the Ceylonese have to live, for these features form the essential background to the tale that must be told and, further, have had not a little influence on the tale itself. This tale will then be taken up in order to demonstrate not only the origins of the various peoples and communities who may be called 'Ceylonese' but also the roots of the myths that the Ceylonese hold about each other, for these have had an important effect on attitudes and conduct. The effects of the move of the centre of gravity of Sinhalese settlement from the Dry Zone to the Wet Zone and the hills will then be examined; and this examination will be followed by an enquiry into the effects on inter-communal relations of the period of colonial rule, Portuguese, Dutch and British. Colonial rule was responsible for a revolution in the economy of Ceylon, and the new economy has many points of contact (which will be identified) with the peoples of Ceylon and the tensions between them. Finally, the present ethnic situation in Ceylon will be described; and the interaction of this situation on politics and of politics on this situation will be examined—for it is this interaction that brings the argument to the point at which, it is hoped, the present communal position in Ceylon will become reasonably clear.

Although this booklet is being published under the auspices of the Institute of Race Relations, I think it better not to describe the peoples of Ceylon (the Sinhalese, the Tamils and the rest) as 'races', a term which I am not alone, of course, in wishing to restrict to groups with recognisable, biologically inheritable differences (like skin colour) in common. Such has been the tangled ethnic history of

Ceylon's peoples and of their ancestors on the Indian mainland that it is extremely doubtful whether it is possible to distinguish, say, a 'Sinhalese racial type' or a 'Tamil racial type'. Certainly there are no obvious racial differences like those between European and African in South Africa. The peoples of Ceylon, however, differ markedly in terms of traditions, culture and attitudes, and accordingly are best described by using terms such as 'people', 'ethnic groups', or 'community'. Differences of caste and religion are also important.

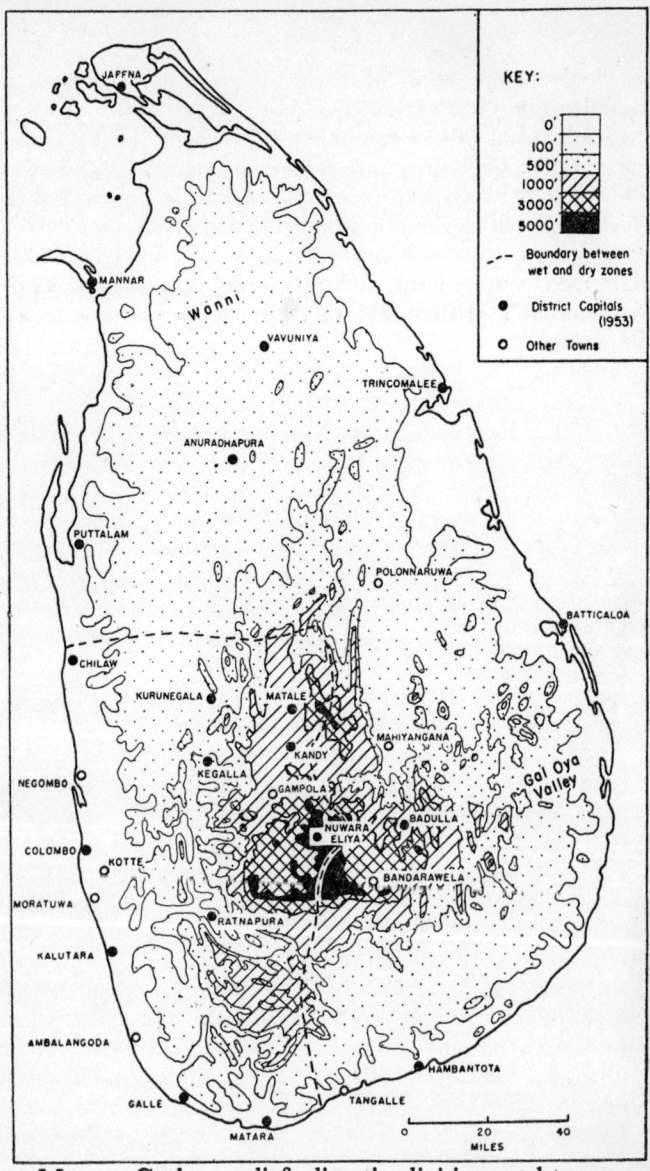

Map 1. Ceylon: relief, climatic divisions and towns.

1. THE LAND OF CEYLON AND ITS PEOPLING: FACT, MYTH AND CONFLICT

CEYLON is a tropical island covering some 25,000 square miles. It is of the same order of size as the Republic of Ireland, or West Virginia, or the Benelux countries. The Sinhalese call it 'Sri Lanka' ('Holy Lanka') and the Tamils 'Ilam' or 'Elankai'.

Within its relatively small compass Ceylon contrives to contain surprising contrasts of scene and of resources which have had a profound influence on its people and on their history. The most important contrast is between the climate of the so-called 'Wet Zone' and that of the so-called 'Dry Zone', a contrast that is almost unbelievably sharp to those who are familiar only with the gradual transitions to be found in temperate islands like Britain or the even more gradual transitions of the great continental interiors. The Wet Zone, which corresponds roughly to the south-western sector of Ceylon (see Map 1), receives at most seasons of the year rainfall that is adequate or more than adequate for plant growth. In earlier times it must for the most part have been covered in dense, tangled tropical rain forest, but this now survives only where protected, as in the Sinharaja Forest Reserve; for most of the Wet Zone is now under cultivation. The climate (except where affected by altitude) suits such commercial crops as rubber and coconuts, and rice grows readily under the combined stimulus of a generally adequate rainfall and of the river-water that can in many places be led easily to the fields and terraces from local streams. Tea flourishes from sea-level up to 5,000 feet or more; indeed, it gains in flavour and profitability with height. The Ceylon Wet Zone is a green, pleasant area, palm-shaded in the lowlands, rich with tea gardens in its hills—the epitome, in fact, of the tropical island as conceived alike by the schoolboy and the film-goer.

If, however, one travels north from Colombo to just beyond Chilaw, or between Matara and Tangalle, or a short distance east from the hill-capital of Kandy, one enters with something of a shock a very different landscape, that of the Dry Zone. The coconuts begin to be a little sickly and soon disappear reappearing only in occasional plantations or in mixed tree-gardens around villages built beside 'tanks' or artificial reservoirs. Tea and rubber disappear altogether. Rice-fields there are, but they clearly cling as to a life-line to channels springing from tanks or other sources of water. And there is still an abundance of jungle, in spite of inroads made upon it at an ever accelerating pace during the past twenty years or so: not the impressive rain forest of Sinharaja, but poorer, scrubbier stuff, green enough when the rains come but in the dry season altogether browner and duller, with plenty of apparently dead branches that have in reality only shed their leaves till the drought is over. For the essence of the Dry Zone character and of the Dry Zone problem (yet paradoxically one of its apparent indirect attractions to early settlement) is the seasonal character of the rainfall. Rain falls most years (though even this is somewhat unreliable) during the period from October to early February. Even less reliable rains *may* fall in September and in March and April. But almost always, all too reliably, there is drought from May to August or longer—intense, searing drought which coincides with the hottest temperatures in the annual cycle, drought which excludes tea and rubber altogether, which only permits coconut where there is water for its feet, which demands irrigation by stored water if rice is to be grown and which kills off unirrigated shallow-rooted crops. This Dry Zone regime, locally modified, rules most of northern and eastern Ceylon, but is to some extent mitigated and modified by altitude in the eastern side of the central hills.

The second source of contrast in Ceylon, unimportant compared with climate, is its relief. Ceylon rises by a series of irregular steps from coastal lowlands to broken highlands, largely over 5,000 feet, which occupy much of the south-centre of the island. There is thus a contrast between lowland (roughly below the 1,000 foot contour, and for the most part gently rolling in general character) and highland, steep and tumbled, often rising from the lowland in a great, wall-like scarp. The highlands are, naturally, cooler than the lowlands but parts of them, notably those facing west, attract very heavy rainfall and correspondingly dense forest.[1]

Today Ceylon is occupied by a varied mixture of peoples. The Sinhalese—themselves often divided, with some justification, into 'Low-Country Sinhalese' and 'Kandyan' (or 'Up-country') 'Sinhalese'—form the majority community, and are concentrated in the Wet Zone, with an important spread also over Raja Rata ('the King's country', round Anurradhapura, the ancient capital) and a thinner scatter in the western and eastern Dry Zone (see Map 2 p. 60). The Ceylon Tamils, descendants of Tamil-speaking immigrants from south India who for the most part came to Ceylon long ago, have their main concentration in the Jaffna peninsula in the far north, a harsh land where the Dry Zone climate is to be found in a form which provides the greatest possible contrast between the rainy and dry seasons, but where water-bearing strata make possible the irrigation of crops by means of wells, a solution denied to most of the Dry Zone for geological reasons. Ceylon Tamils are also to be found in a subsidiary concentration down the east coast, north and south of Batticaloa; in a thinner scatter over the northern Dry Zone (where they march with the Sinhalese in the Puttalam, Vavuniya and Trincomalee Districts); and, nowadays, in government and other employment in many

---

[1] For further detail on the climate, relief and other variable features of Ceylon's physical geography, see B. H. Farmer, 'Ceylon' in O. H. K. Spate, *India and Pakistan* (2nd. ed., London, Methuen, 1957).

other places. Indian Tamils, not to be confused with the Ceylon Tamils, are recent immigrants or the descendants of recent immigrants, brought over to work on plantations in the hills and on their flanks in the Wet Zone. Smaller communities include Moors (Muslims), Burghers (persons of Dutch or mixed descent), Malays and Europeans. Moors form 25 per cent or more of the population in Puttalam, Mannar, Trincomalee and Batticaloa Districts.

The number of people contained in each of the various ethnic groups, according to the 1953 census of Ceylon, was as follows:[2]

Citizens of Ceylon:	Low-Country Sinhalese	3,464,126
	Kandyan Sinhalese	2,157,206
	Total Sinhalese	5,621,332
	Ceylon Tamils	908,705
	Ceylon Moors	468,146
	Malays	28,736
	Burghers	43,916
	Others	20,678
Not Citizens of Ceylon:	Indians (mainly Tamils)	984,327
	Pakistanis	5,749
	Europeans	5,886
	Others	11,162
	TOTAL	8,098,637

The population of Ceylon at the end of 1962 was probably of the order of 11 million, an increase of close on 40 per cent since the 1953 Census. It can therefore be assumed that the Sinhalese community at the end of 1962 numbered about 8 million, and that there were at the same date about $1\frac{1}{4}$ million Ceylon Tamils and rather more than that number of Indian Tamils.

How did this plural society come into being and how did it acquire its present distribution? The history of Ceylon, and in particular the story of its peopling, first acquire a reasonable measure of clarity in the fifth century A.D., the

[2] Source: (Colombo, Department of Census and Statistics, 1953), Table 1.

FACT, MYTH AND CONFLICT 5

period during which an unknown Buddhist monk wrote the *Mahavamsa*, the history, as the chronicler saw it, of the Kings of Ceylon from the earliest time to his own.[3] His chronicle can naturally be most relied on when he is relating events nearest to his own times; but it is also of significance because the way in which he told his tale was to be a strong formative influence on Ceylon's history in general and on communal relations in particular.

Early medieval Ceylon is known from the *Mahavamsa*[4] and from archaeological and other evidence to have had two main nuclei of Sinhalese settlement, both in the lowland Dry Zone, both in areas of relatively good soil, and both dependent on the technical skill in irrigating the Dry Zone which the Sinhalese had by this time acquired. Both, too, show a high level of civilisation and, in particular, of architectural achievement. There were minor settlements in the Wet Zone (notably round the mouth of the Kelani Ganga, not far from the site of modern Colombo) and in the lower hills (especially in the north overlooking Raja Rata); but these regions were not densely settled until much later, perhaps because the early and medieval Sinhalese were deterred by the dense rain-forest and found it easier to clear the lighter vegetation of the Dry Zone, a region which their irrigation techniques enabled them to utilise agriculturally. Irrigation was, in fact, greatly extended during the fifth century A.D., notably by the Sinhalese King Dhatusena, who reigned in Anuradhapura from A.D. 460 to 478 and who built, among other works, the great Kala Wewa. The dam of this tank (now restored and once more pouring forth water into the rice-fields) is three-and-a-half miles long and sends water to Anuradhapura through a channel that winds

---

[3] The *Mahavamsa* is available in English translation; see W. Geiger (trans.) *The Mahavamsa or the Great Chronicle of Ceylon*, new edn. (Colombo, Ceylon Government Information Department, 1950).
[4] For the early history of Ceylon see especially G. C. Mendis, *The Early History of Ceylon* (Ceylon, Y.M.C.A. Publishing House, 1938); and S. Paranavitana (ed.), *The University of Ceylon History of Ceylon*, vol. 1, Parts 1 and 2 (Colombo, Ceylon University Press, 1959 and 1960).

its way through Raja Rata for more than fifty miles. Dhatusena also built many great Buddhist shrines.

Often at this period Ruhuna and Raja Rata were ruled as separate kingdoms; sometimes they were in conflict, sometimes they were united. But these early medieval Sinhalese, though they must have been the majority community, were not left alone in Raja Rata and Ruhuna to enjoy their inheritance undisturbed by foreign invasion. When Dhatusena ascended the throne the Tamils, who had invaded from south India and who may already have been settling in northern Ceylon, were in possession of Anuradhapura. One of Dhatusena's chief claims to fame is that he re-entered the ancient capital as a victorious conqueror after twenty years of struggle.

In Dhatusena's reign, then, there were already Sinhalese firmly established in Ceylon, and there were Tamils too; and already the two communities were in conflict. But the conflict had then, as it has now, overtones that have much to do with the view that the Sinhalese took of their origin, of their peculiar destiny, and of their relationship to the Tamils.

As Professor E. F. C. Ludowyk has recently shown, this is where the *Mahavamsa* and its unknown monkish chronicler come into the picture.[5] The *Mahavamsa*, in the first place, gave the Sinhalese a myth about their origin which, far-fetched as it is, convinced them that they were a people with something special about them. The myth tells of an Indian prince, Vijaya, the grandson of a union between an Indian princess and a lion (hence 'Sinhala', the 'lion race'). Vijaya landed in Ceylon with a band of followers under the protection of the Buddha who, as he entered nirvana in far-off northern India, prayed: 'In Lanka, O Lord of gods, will my religion be established, therefore, carefully protect him with his followers, and Lanka.' Vijaya, after many adventures among the *yakkhas* and *yakkhinis* of the island

[5] E. F. C. Ludowyk, *The Story of Ceylon* (London, Faber, 1962).

(male and female demons, perhaps representing the aboriginal inhabitants of the island) founded a city and a kingdom. Forsaking the *yakkhini* who had born him two children (from whom, one story has it, the jungle peoples, the now-vanishing Vedda, are descended) he took as his queen a princess of a royal Indian house. Thus, in a nutshell, runs the myth in which the Sinhalese saw, and still see, their special origin and identity, and their special character as an Aryan people set far from their homeland among alien and hostile folk.

There can be no doubt that one aspect of this myth has some foundation in fact. The Sinhalese do speak an Aryan tongue, which belongs to the same family as such ancient Indian languages as Sanskrit and Pali and such modern Indian languages as Hindi, Bengali and Marathi. Sinhalese, in fact, is completely different from such Dravidian languages, as Tamil, though modern Sinhalese has, through centuries of contact, borrowed Tamil words. It may well be, then, that a band of people hailing from north of the then frontier of Dravidian speech did somehow arrive in Ceylon some centuries before the birth of Christ, though whether from north-west or from north-east India is not clear. Perhaps separate groups came one from each coast.[6] This is not to say that all of the modern Sinhalese are the descendants, in a pure line, of immigrants from north India. It may well be that, as a recent authority has put it:

The higher culture, including the languages, brought to these regions by the Sinhalese as well as the Tamils, was adopted in varying degrees by the people of a Stone Age culture who were there before their arrival. Thus, the vast majority of the people who today speak Sinhalese or Tamil must ultimately be descended from those autochthonous people of whom we know next to nothing.[7]

---

[6] For a summary of the present state of the controversy over the origin of the Sinhalese, see S. Paranavitana, vol. 1, part 1, pp. 93–97.
[7] *Ibid.*, p. 96.

In other words, it may well be that Sinhalese and Tamils have much in common genetically, their separation being, like so many similar cleavages the world over, primarily a linguistic and cultural one.[8] But it is of great significance that from early times, at least as early as the writing of the *Mahavamsa*, the Sinhalese have thought of themselves as a unique and specially favoured people. It is also of significance that they speak an Aryan tongue, fundamentally different, in spite of borrowings, from Tamil. This fundamental difference has in several different ways exacerbated the language controversies of recent years.

But the Sinhalese conception of themselves as unique and specially-favoured was rooted not only in a myth about their distinctive origin but sprang also from a belief about themselves as the chosen guardians of Buddhism, and about their island, 'Sri Lanka', as a place of special sanctity for the Buddhist religion. Rather as the Old Testament builds up the concept of Israel as a specially chosen people in a way that has had a profound influence on Jews ever since, so does the *Mahavamsa* build up the concept of the special destiny of the Sinhalese kings, the Sinhalese people, and the island of Sri Lanka in relation to Buddhism; and the result has been equally profound.

Sinhalese kings are remembered in the *Mahavamsa* for their fidelity to Buddhism, their support of the priesthood and their religious building; one is constantly reminded of passages about the kings of Israel in the biblical books of Kings and Chronicles. The *Mahavamsa*, too, tells us myths which reinforce the atmosphere of special sanctity it is at such pains to create. There is, for instance, the myth that tells how the Buddha himself, knowing 'that in the midst of Lanka, on the fair river bank, in the delightful Mahanaga garden ... there was a great gathering of all the yakkhas dwelling in the island', was transported through the air to Lanka, and made many converts. This visit to the site of

---

[8] In addition, certain Sinhalese castes may well have originated in the immigration of Tamils (see below, pp. 26 and 31).

FACT, MYTH AND CONFLICT 9

the present Mahiyangana temple was, according to the myth, followed by two more to other places in Ceylon.

Later in the *Mahavamsa*, after the story of Vijaya and his immediate successors, there is related the charming story of Mahinda, son of Asoka. Mahinda arrived through the air to land on the hill at Mihintale, east of Anuradhapura, where he encountered and converted the King Devanampiyatissa, who had gone hunting on the mountain. Mahinda's preaching of the *dhamma* was miraculously heard all over the island; and Mahinda, 'like unto the Master in the protection of Lanka, ... preached the true doctrine ... in the speech of the island' and this 'brought to pass the descent of the true faith'.[9]

Thus in the myths that the *Mahavamsa* makes to surround the landing of Vijaya and the arrival of the Buddha and of Buddhism are intertwined already the religion, the national identity and the language of the Sinhalese. And this triple intertwining has characterised the Sinhalese as it has characterised the Jewish people, with equally significant results in terms of contemporary affairs.

But, before we leave the *Mahavamsa*, we must introduce the question of its attitude to the Tamils who were already, at the time the chronicle was being written, invading the holy island and possibly even settling in it. To some extent the Tamils are cast in the role of the Philistines, 'good' Kings being those who, like Dutthagamani, smote the Tamils hip and thigh, and did so, partly at least, with religious motives. 'Not for the joy of sovereignty is this toil of mine', Dutthagamani (161–137 B.C.) is made to say in the midst of one of his campaigns, 'my striving has been ever to establish the doctrine of the Sambuddha'.[10] After a long war, graphically described in the *Mahavamsa*, Dutthagamani finally arrived at the gates of the ancient capital, the sacred city of Buddhism, Anuradhapura. In a great battle many Tamils ('Damilas') were killed, and the

[9] *Ibid.*, p. 96.
[10] *Ibid.*, p. 171

Tamil King, Elara, fled towards the city. There, near the south gate, the two Kings, one Sinhalese, the other Tamil, engaged in heroic single combat. 'Elara hurled his dart, Gamani evaded it; he made his own elephant pierce Elara's elephant with his tusks and he hurled his dart at Elara; and this latter fell there, with his elephant'.[11] Then, after a further battle, all the Tamils being slain, Dutthagamani sat on the terrace of his palace in the sacred city 'adorned, lighted with fragrant lamps and filled with many a perfume, magnificent with nymphs in the guise of dancing girls' and 'looking back upon his glorious victory, great though it was, knew no joy, remembering that thereby was wrought the destruction of millions [*sic*]'.[12] There came through the air, however, eight *arahants* [creatures no longer subject to rebirth] and comforted the King in his remorse by saying to him 'From this deed arises no hindrance on thy way to heaven. Only one and a half human beings have been slain here by thee, O lord of men. The one had come unto the three refuges [i.e., was a Buddhist], the other had taken on himself the five precepts [i.e., was half-way to being a Buddhist]. Unbelievers and men of evil life were the rest, not more to be esteemed than beasts.'[13] Thus, the cynic may say, did the Church rationalise away the moral feelings of the King. Dutthagamani emerges not only as *Fidei Defensor* but as an aggressive campaigner for Buddhism who for his pains wins himself eighty-one out of the 271 pages in the *Mahavamsa*. A fairer estimate would perhaps have it that religion, kingship and the fate of the Sinhalese nation are once again demonstrated to be inextricably interwoven. Certainly Dutthagamani became a great warrior-hero in the minds of his people. Through his efforts and the efforts of others like him (notably the King Dhatusena, see pp. 5–6 above) the Sinhalese were saved from absorption by Tamil powers in south India; and,

[11] *Ibid.*, p. 175.
[12] *Ibid.*, p. 177.
[13] *Ibid.*, pp. 177–8.

FACT, MYTH AND CONFLICT

during a period in which Buddhism was in full retreat on the mainland in the face of a resurgent Hinduism, it remained the dominant religion in Ceylon. Moreover, when in the fullness of time there was no longer a threat from the Tamils of south India, but nonetheless a Tamil kingdom was firmly established in lands of Tamil settlement round Jaffna in the north of Ceylon, 'a special quality of hostility could be elicited'[14] among the Sinhalese at times of conflict and stress because of what they knew of their history (as the *Mahavamsa* told it) and because of the position as warrior-heroes of men like Dutthagamani and Dhatusena.

But this is not to say that Tamils and Sinhalese were always in conflict, nor that the Tamils do not sometimes, even in the pages of the *Mahavamsa*, appear in a better guise than that of 'unbelievers and men of evil life ... not more to be esteemed than beasts'. The King, Elara, is said by the *Mahavamsa* to have ruled 'with even justice toward friend and foe' and 'at the head of his bed' to have had 'a bell with a long rope hung up so that those who desired a judgement at law might ring it'.[15] He is, further, said to have been 'a protector of [Buddhist] tradition', 'albeit, he knew not the peerless virtues of the most precious of the three gems', and to have had miraculous powers because, although he had not put aside 'false beliefs' he had 'freed himself from walking in the path of evil'. And Dutthagamani, after Elara had been slain, personally celebrated the dead King's funeral rites, and built a monument at which he ordained worship; 'even to this day', says the *Mahavamsa* 'the princes of Lanka, when they draw near to this place, are wont to silence their music because of this worship'.[16]

It is important, indeed, to stress that tolerance has often been not only a Buddhist but a Sinhalese virtue. In the words of Abu Zeid al Hasan who visited Ceylon in the

[14] E. F. C. Ludowyk, p. 65.
[15] *Mahavamsa*, p. 143.
[16] *Ibid.*, p. 175.

ninth century A.D., 'In this same island there is a very great multitude of Jews, as well as of many other sects, even Tanwis or Manichees, the King permitting the free exercise of every Religion'.[17] There have been many occasions since when religious tolerance has been very much in evidence, and when Sinhalese and Tamils have lived together in the same village in harmony. But, nevertheless, the communal relationship was, like that which appears to be implicit in the *Mahavamsa*, possessed by a certain ambivalence; the 'special quality of hostility' was always liable to be called forth in times of stress; and for this the *Mahavamsa* must take much of the blame: it is recognisably because of the way that the tale is told in it that the modern Buddhist scholar, the Bhikkhu Rahula, is able to say that Dutthagamani's war was 'a great crusade to liberate Buddhism from foreign rule' and, to continue:

His war-cry was 'Not for kingdom but for Buddhism'. The entire Sinhalese race was united under the banner of young Gamani. This was the beginning of nationalism among the Sinhalese. It was a new race with healthy young blood, organized under the new order of Buddhism. A kind of religio-nationalism, which almost amounted to fanaticism, roused the whole Sinhalese people. A non-Buddhist was not regarded as a human being. Evidently all Sinhalese without exception were Buddhists.[18]

For centuries after the writing of the *Mahavamsa* in the fifth century A.D. and after the campaigns of Dhatusena (A.D. 460–478) the identification of Buddhism with the Sinhalese kingdom continued; so did persistent invasions from south India, often by Tamils, sometimes by other peoples such as Keralas. Though Tamils were not infrequently brought in as mercenaries by warring Sinhalese,

---

[17] Quoted in E. K. Cook, revised K. Kularatnam, *Ceylon* (London, Macmillan, 1951), p. 7.
[18] From Bhikkhu Rahula, *History of Buddhism in Ceylon: The Anuradhapura Period* (Colombo, Gumasena, 1956), quoted by E. F. C. Ludowyk, op. cit., p. 64.

civilisation is revived from time to time. In the *Culavamsa*,[19] which continues the story from the *Mahavamsa*, Parakkamabahu I plays the part assigned to Dutthagamani in the earlier chronicle. Having dealt with various internecine feuds and rebellions, he cleared Anuradhapura of Tamils. The sacred city 'had been utterly destroyed in every way by the Cola army', and Parakkamabahu set Tamil prisoners to work on restorations.

Parakkamabahu's own capital was, however, at Polonnaruwa, and the move to the more southerly site was significant. Gradually over the centuries, with occasional oscillations to a more northerly situation, the capital of the Sinhalese kingdom moved south to avoid the invasion-swept territory that had once been Raja Rata. By the thirteenth century the capital, and presumably also the centre of gravity of Sinhalese settlement, had moved into the Wet Zone; by the fourteenth century the capital was at Gampola, and the Sinhalese kingdom, in sad decline, had abandoned its sacred cities and split into a shifting pattern of fragments. In the far north a Tamil 'King' reigned in Jaffna. When Europeans came to Ceylon late in the fifteenth century they found a pattern very different from that of classical Sinhalese times. Most of the Dry Zone was derelict apart from the Jaffna Peninsula and strips along the east and west coasts, where Tamil settlers found conditions not unlike those to which they were used in south India. Where the great shrines of Anuradhapura and Polonnaruwa had risen proudly and splendidly there were only jungle-covered ruins; where great tanks and channels had irrigated thousands of acres and supported what must have been a fairly large population there were only small, malarial villages huddling near small, surviving tanks. Large areas were almost devoid of population; this applied particularly to the region north of the old Raja Rata, which became known as

[19] W. Geiger (trans.), *Culavamsa, being the More Recent Part of the Mahavamsa*, 2 vols., new edn. (Colombo, Ceylon Government Information Department, 1953).

the *Wanni*, the jungle, and which for a long time, with comparable areas inland from the west and east coast of the Dry Zone, provided something of a marchland between Sinhalese and Tamils. The main centres of Sinhalese population were, anyway, far to the south, in the Wet Zone and in the lower hills; here, amid sadly decadent architecture, the old connexion of Buddhism and kingship was maintained; and, no doubt, myths of former greatness and of the evils brought on Sri Lanka by the Tamils were nurtured.

Certainly in modern times a popular view in Ceylon has been that the decline and fall of ancient Sinhalese civilisation was brought about by the Tamils, who are sometimes alleged deliberately to have destroyed the irrigation works on which, given the Dry Zone environment, settlement so clearly depended. It may well be that the repeated Tamil invasions, coupled with anarchy within the Sinhalese kingdoms themselves, had much to do with the decay that so manifestly set in. But there is no evidence of deliberate destruction. The damage wrought in Dry Zone irrigation works by the great floods of December 1957 and January 1958 demonstrated what Nature in the Dry Zone can do; and it would only have needed a breakdown in administration, such as must have occurred in the period in question, to allow Nature a free hand.

Malaria, too, may well have played its part. In modern times, until control by D.D.T., malaria has hung over the Dry Zone like a pall. Only one vector, *Anopheles culicifacies*, is known; this breeds in sunlit pools such as those into which the Dry Zone rivers decline in the dry season, so that the Dry Zone environment provides an ideal home for this species of mosquito. In modern times malaria in the Dry Zone kept population static or declining, and pitifully inactive. It is inconceivable that such a malaria-ridden population could have achieved the marvels of ancient Ceylon. Perhaps, then, malaria first came to Ceylon at about the time of the final decline of its ancient civilisation, and helped to depopulate the Dry Zone and to leave the half-empty marchland across which Tamils and Sinhalese faced each other at the beginning of European contact.

II. FOUR HUNDRED AND FIFTY YEARS OF FOREIGN RULE: THE PORTUGUESE AND THE DUTCH

ON 15 November 1505 the *baxels* (large sailing ships) of Dom Lourenco da Almeida, having been blown off course while bound for the Maldive Islands, sailed into the embayment which has now become Colombo harbour, and made contact with the King of Kotte, six miles inland. His men carved the arms of Portugal on a rock which may still be seen in the public garden near Queen's House, the residence of the British Governors of Ceylon and now that of the Governor-General. Thus was initiated those '450 years of foreign rule' which were to end with the coming of independence on 4 February 1948 and on which modern Ceylonese nationalists are apt to blame all the shortcomings of their country and their countrymen, with very much the sort of universal condemnation that Hilaire Belloc poured on the Reformation (to which, it may be remembered, he attributed 'determinism, capitalism, socialism, vegetarianism, teetotalism, and other afflictions').

Whatever be the truth about the general effects of the era of imperialism, it cannot be denied that the rule of the Portuguese and of their successors in Ceylon, the Dutch and the British, had such important results on the distribution of peoples and on the communal situation that the Ceylon scene was altered out of all recognition. Seldom, however, were such changes the result of deliberate policy: rather were they by-products of foreign rule, especially of its economic aspects.

The Portuguese were at first interested primarily in trade, especially in cinnamon, of which Ceylon was the sole source. They gradually extended their rule over the Wet Zone lowlands, over the Mannar area, and over the northern

Tamil kingdom of Jaffna—partly by conquest, partly because the last King of Kotte, the ruler of one of the petty states into which the Sinhalese dominion had fragmented and the claimant to suzerainty over the whole island, made the Portuguese King his heir, so that when he died in 1597 the Portuguese were able to lay claim to the whole island. They also set up trading stations or forts outside their western and northern territory at such places as Trincomalee and Batticaloa. But, in spite of a number of expeditions, punitive and otherwise, they never succeeded in conquering the hill kingdom centred on Kandy, nor the territories which it claimed and which stretched far north into the old Raja Rata and east to the Bay of Bengal. Finally, in 1658, after a period of conflict and uncertainty, the last Portuguese troops left Ceylon and the Dutch ruled in their stead.

The Portuguese caught Sinhalese civilisation when it was already fast disintegrating. Gone were the glories of ancient days in Raja Rata, abandoned to the jungle were many of the great shrines of former times. The process of decay and of fragmentation had been in train long before Dom Lourenco's accidental landfall, and it might well have gone much further had the Portuguese never come to Ceylon. But it cannot be doubted that, by playing off one petty ruler of a broken kingdom against his rivals, they hastened disintegration and ensured that for a long time ahead unity of the Sinhalese kingdom and nation would be out of the question. Because they were an alien and a conquering people they were, in the fullness of time, blamed together with their imperial successors for much that might have happened anyway; and because of the nature of their ancient chronicles the Sinhalese, or some of them, were to look back to a Golden Age which had been lost, not because of their own faults, but because of Tamil and European intervention: a Golden Age in which the Sinhalese kingdom, the Sinhalese language and Sinhalese Buddhism had all flourished exceedingly and in such intimate association that an attack on one was construed as an attack on all three.

So much for the general effect of Portuguese intervention in Ceylon. Of their particular and ethnic effects, one of the most far-reaching was the beginning of the process of differentiation between Low-Country and Kandyan Sinhalese. It is highly significant that to this day the Low-Country Sinhalese are those inhabiting the territories which Portugal either conquered or acquired by inheriting the Kotte kingdom, less those for the most part already inhabited by Tamils or Moors at the time of Portuguese contact: the Low-Country Sinhalese, in other words, are those living in the lowlands of the Wet Zone, from Chilaw in the north to Hambantota in the south. The Kandyan Sinhalese, on the other hand, are those living in lands which the Portuguese never conquered, or at least never held for long: lands in the central highlands and in the Dry Zone short of the areas of Tamil settlement. The Kandyans not surprisingly retained, and to a considerable extent still retain, a social system relatively unaffected by European contact in terms of, for instance, caste, religion, or the position of the land-owning aristocracy. Not surprisingly, too, they tend to regard themselves as the true heirs to the traditions of immemorial Sinhalese civilisation, the guardians of Buddhism (is not the sacred tooth relic in Kandy to this day?) and, unlike the Low-Country Sinhalese (whom they tend to despise) uncorrupted by the West. I remember the case of the daughter of an aristocratic Kandyan family whose marriage to a Low-Countryman of the same caste was opposed by certain of her aunts on the grounds that 'No Purānagama has ever married below Kadugannawa' (I have chosen a fictional village-name to conceal the name of friends because aristocratic Kandyan families commonly take their name from that of their ancestral village: Kadugannawa is a village guarding a spectacular pass, used by the modern road and railway, which lies well inside Kandyan territory, but was chosen by the kings of Kandy as a main defensive position guarding the innermost core of their kingdom).

The Low-Country Sinhalese, on the other hand, were drawn by the Portuguese and their successors into the main stream of world commerce. Many elements of their social system, notably caste, religion and land tenure were subject to rapid and often disintegrating change (more will be said about caste and religion as ethnically divisive forces in a moment). Many Low-Country Sinhalese took Portuguese names like de Silva, Fernando, de Fonseca and Pereira (or Perera), partly no doubt because of the prestige thereby acquired, partly also to conceal caste, which is nearly always given away by traditional names. This process has continued into recent times. The father of a friend of mine whose *ge* or family name was Hettihewage, a Salāgama caste-name (see below p. 31) took the name de Silva when he entered the service of the British colonial Government, ostensibly to make it easier for his new masters to address him, really to conceal his caste on moving from his old village to a post elsewhere. This very mobility was in itself, of course, a new feature, dating back to the Portuguese but not before. Some Low-Country Sinhalese who did not take Portuguese surnames nevertheless used such first names as 'Don Stephen' to indicate (ostensibly) that 'Don' was an hereditary title conferred by the Portuguese. D. S. Senanayake, the first Prime Minister of independent Ceylon, was in fact Don Stephen Senanayake. (It should perhaps be noted that Low-Country aristocrats do not ordinarily use the name of their ancestral village as a personal name, though in recent years there has been some tendency in this direction: 'Peiris' has, for example, become 'Deraniyagala').

Fashions in family names are unimportant in themselves, of course; but they are a symptom of what, from the Kandyan viewpoint, is a serious *malaise* in Low-Country Sinhalese society—a tendency to ape the West and to yield to it instead of guarding the integrity of traditional civilisation. That this feature (which clearly serves to draw an ethnic boundary between Low-Country and Kandyan Sinhalese) goes back to Portuguese times is evident from the fact that it is almost invariably Portuguese names that have been adopted.

The prevalence of Portuguese names in Low-Country Ceylon has misled many Western visitors into exaggerating the extent both of Portuguese intermarriage and of Portuguese conversions to Roman Catholicism. The truth is that many bearers of Portuguese names are Buddhist, and that the Portuguese contribution to the genetic stock of Ceylon is indeterminate, but probably not very significant. It is known, of course, that the Portuguese encouraged some of their soldiery and others to intermarry with the local population, since this was held to make for greater security. There may thus be genes of Portuguese origin abroad in the Sinhalese population in consequence; but at least some descendants of mixed marriages became the community eventually known as 'Portuguese Burghers' who, despised alike by the Sinhalese, the Dutch and the British, degenerated and took on what are by Sinhalese standards essentially low-caste occupations as shoe-makers, tailors, blacksmiths and artisans generally. Today this community is of little significance and is politically unorganised; it tends to merge with the poverty-stricken, rootless Sinhalese of the Colombo slums.

The Portuguese, it will be remembered, put down the Tamil kingdom of Jaffna and included its territories, or some of them, in its domain. In the Jaffna peninsula itself the Portuguese had something of the effect that they had in the lowland Wet Zone, differentiating the peninsula from other areas of Tamil settlement and launching it into the stream of Westernisation. But, so far as can be judged, their effect was not as great as among the Low-Country Sinhalese; certainly Jaffna Tamils do not appear to have taken Portuguese surnames, though those who were baptised took Christian names.

The Portuguese had a considerable effect on the fortunes and distribution of the Muslims whom they found in Ceylon and whom they called 'Moors' a name that has persisted; the Sinhalese name is 'marakkala-minisu' ('seafaring people'). There is a long history of contact with Ceylon on the part of Arab traders, going back to the period of Dry Zone civilisation, and it seems clear that communities of them gathered in seaports and elsewhere. In due course the visiting Arabs had become Muslims; they grew interested in the gems of the Ratnapura area and are known to have settled in Mannar (where the Moorish community is still strong—see Map 2 p. 60) before Portuguese contact. Contemporary accounts seem to show that Muslims were free to practise their religion but were expected to do so without hurting the feelings of the Sinhalese Buddhists.[1] On the other hand, the dominating commercial position which they had won for themselves among a singularly uncommercial people tended to arouse some of the feelings which medieval Christendom felt for the Jews. 'There is no place where the Moorman and the crow cannot be found', runs a proverb in both Sinhalese and Tamil. The Moorish community was undoubtedly both prosperous and powerful during the period of chaos and disintegration that overtook Sinhalese civilisation after it had migrated to the Wet Zone, and Emerson Tennent went so far as to assert that 'But for the timely appearance of a Christian power in the Island Ceylon, instead of being a possession of the British Crown might at the present day [1859] have been a Mahometan Kingdom under the rule of some Arabian adventurer.'[2]

The Portuguese were disposed to be hostile towards the Moors, not only because they were their chief rivals in trade and not inconsiderable adversaries in combat, but also because they were Muslim and hence identified with the

---

[1] S. Paranavitana, vol. I, part II, p. 769.
[2] Sir J. Emerson Tennent, *Ceylon* (London, Longmans, 1859), vol. I, p. 609.

Moors who for so long dominated the Iberian Peninsula. Colombo was besieged by the Moors in 1517, and just over 100 years later the Portuguese Captain-General, Constantino de Sa de Noronha, expelled the Moors from his territories on the orders of King Philip of Spain (by this time also King of Portugal). Some of the Moorish refugees were in turn settled by the Kandyan King in the coastlands of the Batticaloa District, an early piece of Dry Zone recolonisation that is in part at least responsible for the concentration of Moors in the Batticaloa district at present. They form 39 per cent of the population there and are for the most part Tamil-speaking. But, given the seafaring nature of the Moormen, one would expect there to have been Moorish settlement on the east coast before the seventeenth century resettlement, and the Portuguese must not therefore be held entirely responsible for the present distribution of the Moors.

Most Moorish communities today use Tamil as their spoken language, though recent attempts to impose Sinhalese as the national language of Ceylon has to some extent affected adversely the position of Tamil among the Moors. But the traditional preference for Tamil is not a consequence of the seventeenth century plantation of Moors among the east coast Tamils. According to Moorish tradition the community hailed from south India, and it seems reasonably certain that, whatever the extent of actual Arab influence, many Moors who came to Ceylon were in fact the products of the conversion of, or of intermarriage with, Tamils in in India or Ceylon. Many marriages and other customs among the Moors are also based on Tamil practice.

In spite of Portuguese conflict with the Moors it is hardly correct to call them, as H. W. Codrington did, 'the inveterate enemies of the Portuguese'.[3] As E. B. Denham pointed out in one of the many scholarly passages in his review of the census of Ceylon held in 1911, 'the Portuguese

[3] H. W. Codrington, *A Short History of Ceylon* (London, Macmillan, revd. edn., 1939), p. 113.

... were not disposed to interfere with the trade carried on by the Moormen as long as they were not in active opposition'.[4] On some occasions Moors fought for the Portuguese against the Sinhalese, and one Portuguese, described them as 'the only ones in India in whom we never found deceit'.

Much more important than the Portuguese impact on the Moors in its effects on the present social and political situation were the efforts of the Portuguese to convert the Sinhalese and others to Roman Catholicism. There are in fact more Christians than Muslims in Ceylon, and more of them are Roman Catholics than adherents of any other Christian denomination. There is a tradition of the existence of Nestorian Christianity in Ceylon in the time of Justinian, and St. Thomas the Apostle is said to have visited the island; but whatever the truth behind these and other traditions it was the Portuguese who first effectively propagated Christianity in Ceylon. This they did by all the means in their power and, as Sydney Bailey has said, 'the energy, zeal and fanaticism of the Portuguese in their efforts to secure converts is well known'.[5] The Portuguese Viceroy was charged by his King to 'discover all the idols ... to reduce them to fragments and utterly to consume them', and to encourage conversions through the granting of temporal favours, such as remission of taxes, as well as through 'conviction of the purity of the faith'. Not for nothing do the Portuguese civil and military authorities, together with the religious orders so active in Portuguese times, stand charged with propagating 'a bigoted and arrogant faith, as contemptuous of paganism as it was of Islam'.[6] But there were also occasions when priests and friars protected their flock against the excesses of the soldiery; and whole communities of their converts held to their faith in spite of the loss of their clergy and of persecution in Dutch times.

[4] E. B. Denham, *Ceylon at the Census of 1911* (Colombo, Government Printer, 1912), pp. 234–5.
[5] Sydney D. Bailey, *Ceylon* (London, Hutchinson, 1952), p. 42.
[6] E. F. C. Ludowyk, p. 115.

Such communities tended, however, to be restricted both in geographical location and in caste, with important consequences in modern social and political affairs. It is dangerous to draw conclusions about the long-term effectiveness of Portuguese conversions from the modern census returns, for later missionary activity has also been at work. But it is highly significant that, although the Portuguese baptised a number of people of rank and consequence (notably the King of Kotte who became Don Juan Dharmapala on his baptism), very few Roman Catholics survived inland or among the higher castes. Roman Catholics today form a relatively high proportion of the population in such coastal localities as Mannar, Puttalam and Moratuwa (see Map 1) and in Colombo itself. They form a majority of the population in a coastal strip running from Chilaw to Colombo, and there can be no doubt that the foundation of their strength in this strip was laid in Portuguese times.

Although Ceylon's census returns do not give the population on a caste basis, it is probable that most of the Roman Catholics in this strip, and a fair number in its prolongation southwards along the Wet Zone coast, belong to the fisher caste known among the Sinhalese as 'Karāva'. Before the origins and implications of this state of affairs are discussed, a word ought to be said about caste in Ceylon so far as it is related to the theme of this booklet. Ceylon Tamil society has a modified form of the Hindu caste system to be found across Palk Strait on the mainland of India;[7] beneath the Brahmans (priests) come the Vellālas (cultivators and landlords), the dominating caste politically; Koviyars (servants of Vellālas and petty cultivators); barbers, washermen and others of lower caste including Untouchables. In discussing caste in Jaffna, Michael Banks makes a point that will be readily appreciated by readers of this booklet—that one should not attempt to derive all the traits

[7] See M. Banks, 'Caste in Jaffna' in E. R. Leach (ed.), *Aspects of Caste in South India, Ceylon and North-West Pakistan*, Cambridge Papers in Social Anthropology No. 2 (1960), pp. 61–77.

of the Ceylon Tamil caste system from that of south India. The Tamil/Sinhalese frontier has moved back and forth across the Jaffna Peninsula, and 'whatever may be the current of to-day's cultural drift towards an increasing separation of Tamil and Sinhalese social organisation, it is reading history backwards to suppose that a sharp cleavage has always existed'.[8]

Sinhalese Buddhist society also has its caste system, which tends to survive conversions to Christianity. It differs from at least north Indian caste systems in a number of respects. There are no castes corresponding to the Brahmans (priests) nor to the Ksshatriyas (warriors), though certain castes claim a Ksshatriya origin. The Goyigama or cultivator caste forms both the most numerous and the most-esteemed caste; Goyigama are often equated with Tamil Vellāla both by Sinhalese and Tamils, an interesting example of the relationship of the two societies in spite of their recurrent hostilities. The traditional aristocracy, the Bandāras or Radalas, form a sub-caste of the Goyigama. Below the Goyigama come many other castes, none, however, having the numerical preponderance or the status of the Goyigama. These include the Karāva (originally fishermen), Salāgama (cinnamon-peelers), Durāva (toddy-tappers), Navandanna (artisans, including smiths of all kinds), Hēna (washermen), and many others; there are also, in Kandyan areas, Rodiya who are generally reckoned to be 'out-caste', but 'untouchability' has nothing like the significance in Ceylon that it has in India. The Sinhalese caste system is full of interest, but the temptation to give a fuller account of it here and to compare it with the better-known systems of the Indian mainland must be resisted;[9] discussion will have to

[8] *Ibid.*, p. 61.
[9] The reader is referred to Bryce Ryan, *Caste in Modern Ceylon: the Sinhalese System in Transition* (New Brunswick, N.J. Rutgers University Press, 1953) and to Nur Yalman, 'The Flexibility of Caste Principles in a Kandyan Community' in E. R. Leach (ed.), op. cit., pp. 78–112. For a recent view of the Indian situation see Taya Zinkin, *Caste Today* London, Oxford University Press for the Institute of Race Relations, 1962).

be restricted to ways in which the evolution of the Sinhalese caste system has complicated communal relations or helped to create new tensions or cleavages in society on a national or regional rather than a village scale. One such case is that of the development of the Karāva caste from Portuguese days onwards, and to this case we must now return.

In spite of pretensions to the contrary by certain Karāva writers, it seems likely that the original Karāva were relatively late arrivals from south India who adopted Buddhism and the Sinhalese language (though there is mixed usage of Sinhalese and Tamil among some members of the caste in the Chilaw and Negombo areas). They accordingly present an example of the impossibility of drawing a hard and fast line between Sinhalese and Tamils and, even more, the impossibility of thinking of the racial purity of either linguistic community. The Karāva were fishermen, and many members of the caste still follow their ancestral calling. The Karāva, to a greater extent than any other Sinhalese caste, became Roman Catholics in Portuguese times and retained their faith through subsequent periods of neglect and persecution. Bryce Ryan writes of the reasons for their ready conversion:

Undoubtedly this is a product of coastal position and is perhaps related to their less firm enmeshment in the Sinhalese feudal order and hence greater susceptibility to foreign influences. Secondarily it may be significant that as takers of life their position in reference to Buddhist doctrine is insecure, though this has been exaggerated by early observers.[10]

It may perhaps be added that their 'less firm enmeshment in the Sinhalese feudal order' may have been a result not only of their late arrival and Tamil origins and consequently their dissociation from the ancient tradition uniting Buddhism and Sinhalese national character, but also of the fact, almost a universal experience where religious conversions are concerned, that those with least to lose in the existing order are most readily won to new faiths.

[10] Byce Ryan, p. 105.

Whatever the reasons for the winning of so many Karāva to Roman Catholicism, the consequences have been important. Not only was there, from Portuguese times on, a religious as well as a caste factor tending to divide Catholic Karāva from Sinhalese Buddhists; there was also the effect of Portuguese discrimination in favour of converts to Christianity. This, combined with the advantages of coastal location and with freedom from traditional attitudes hostile to trading, put some Karāva at least on the bottom rungs of a ladder which has led to affluence, and to a place in the country's commerce which has raised the status of the caste to a place in the hierarchy undreamed of by the humble coastal fishermen of the early sixteenth century. This unintentional effect of the Portuguese on the caste situation (which was shared by one or two other coastal castes and which virtually created a new community in Sinhalese society) stands in contrast to deliberate Portuguese policy inland, which on the whole tended to underwrite the existing order, including the caste structure, as a means to political and economic control.

A Sinhalese proverb has it that 'We gave pepper and in exchange got ginger', and refers to the fact that in an effort to be rid of the Portuguese the Kandyan kings enlisted the support of the Dutch, only to find that when the Portuguese were finally expelled in 1658 they had merely succeeded in placing themselves in an equally uncomfortable position. In some ways, indeed, the Dutchman's hand was firmer; though in those which affect the subject-matter of this booklet, Dutch influence was on the whole not as important as that of their predecessors. In any case it may be discussed more briefly, for in a number of ways the influence of the Dutch may be considered an extension or a modification of what had already been achieved by the Portuguese.[11] Like the Portuguese, they never succeeded in

[11] See K. W. Goonewardena, *The Foundation of Dutch Power in Ceylon, 1638–1658* (Amsterdam, Djambatan, 1958); and S. Arasaratnam, *Dutch Power in Ceylon, 1658–1697* (Amsterdam, Djambatan, 1958).

subduing the Kandyan Sinhalese kingdom in spite of a great deal of conflict and a number of expeditions. They effectively controlled and had considerable influence on the territory that had fallen to the Portuguese, namely the Low-Country Wet Zone behind Colombo, Galle and Matara (where they had forts and trading stations), with an extension eastwards to include what is now Hambantota District; the Jaffna peninsula, with Mannar Island; and the marchland of the Wanni, an almost uninhabited territory, to the south. They also had a more tenuous control over the east coast belt and the Chilaw and Puttalam areas. The Dutch were, of course, primarily interested in trade, notably in cinnamon and areca nuts in the Wet Zone and in elephants in the Wanni. Their general effect, therefore, was to develop the trade, commerce and urban growth of their territories, with many consequences for the inhabitants; and thus further to widen the gap between the relatively Westernised and commercialised Low Country and Jaffna Peninsula on the one hand and the Kandyan territory on the other. In particular, they were responsible for further differentiating Low-Country Sinhalese from Kandyan Sinhalese. As E.F.C. Ludowyk puts it:

By the end of the eighteenth century the sharpest contrast existed between life in the small Dutch territories and in the Kandyan country, which after one hundred and fifty years of war against the Portuguese and long continued economic blockade by the Dutch had been reduced to a state of ruinous penury.[12]

That is not to say, however, that the Kandyan country remained completely isolated, nursing its ancient grievances and looking back to its former glories when, according to the chronicles, Buddhism, the monarchy and the Sinhalese language had in splendid combination produced a civilisation around sacred sites now lost to the jungle, the Tamils and the Dutch. For trade had penetrated the Kandyan kingdom, and the Low-Country Karāva were to be found

[12] E. F. C. Ludowyk, p. 129.

purveying salt and dried fish and, in the fullness of time, organising what was virtually the royal transport department which helped to beat the Dutch blockade.[13] This hitherto lowly and coastal caste thus gained in both status and mobility. The Salāgama caste (of whom more in a moment) also began to work up-country in the cinnamon trade.

And, for all the penury and decay in the Kandyan kingdom, and for all the disputed successions and palace intrigues, Kandy kept alive the tradition of the connexion between Buddhism and the monarchy. Indeed, in the middle of the eighteenth century there came a remarkable religious revival. New priests were obtained from Siam and Burma 'to infuse new life into the decadent Buddhist hierarchy',[14] and the King, Kirti Sri, repaired temples, had religious manuscripts copied and devoutly visited shrines. The revival was all the more remarkable (and, some would say, in view of modern developments, ironical) because Kirti Sri was in fact a Tamil, the brother of the Indian senior consort of the last truly Sinhalese King of Ceylon, who died in 1739. Perhaps Kirti Sri's motives were those of some non-Buddhists of modern times, who have been determined to keep their places in seats of power by demonstrating that they are more Buddhist than the Buddhists. Perhaps however, this is merely, one further example of the way in which Sinhalese and Tamil history has been intertwined, for all the fateful divisions of recent years.

In the Low Country one of the effects of the Dutch was the introduction of new communities. The Dutch enlisted in their military, commercial and administrative service many Dutchmen and other Europeans, some of whom settled in Ceylon. One group of these settlers, the 'Dutch Burghers', claim pure European descent and are at pains to deny that they have intermarried with Sinhalese or Tamils.

---

[13] R. Pieris, *Sinhalese Social Organisation* (Colombo, Ceylon University Press Board, 1956), p. 176.
[14] Sydney D. Bailey, p. 63.

Other Burghers do not make or at any rate cannot substantiate any such claim, and in other parts of Asia would be known as Eurasians.

The Dutch also directly affected the ethnic composition of the population of Ceylon in a number of other ways. For example, they introduced Javanese, Amboinese and other Indonesians as, for instance, soldiers. This is the origin of the so-called 'Malay' community in Ceylon, which in spite of much intermarriage retains its identity and its Muslim religion.[15] It numbered 28,736 according to the 1953 census. Nearly half of these were in Colombo, especially in the district known as 'Slave Island', and a much smaller group formed nearly a quarter of the population of the small town of Hambantota. The Dutch also moved Tamils from Tanjore, together with 'citizens of Colombo', into lands inland from that city which had been denuded of population during the long struggle with the Kandyan King. It is interesting to speculate how Tamil are the 'Sinhalese' inhabitants of some of these areas today.

The Moors did not incur the fanatical religious hostility of the Dutch as they had of the Portuguese; but the Dutch resented strongly what they regarded as interference with their trading monopoly and subjected them to a number of irksome regulations: they were, for instance, forbidden to reside within the commercial areas of places like Colombo, Galle and Matara;

> Only agriculture and navigation must be left open to them as occupations, and they are prohibited from engaging in all other trades within this country, either directly or indirectly. And with a view to gradually exterminate [sic] this impudent class of people Their Honours have prohibited any increase to their numbers from outside.[16]

[15] Malays also entered the service of the King of Kandy.
[16] Sophia Pieters (trans.), *Instructions from the Governor-General and Council of India to the Governor of Ceylon, 1656 to 1665* (Colombo, Government Printer, 1908), pp. 63–4.

But very few of these restrictive measures seem to have had much effect on the distribution or character of the Moorish community, not least because the Dutch attitude towards them was ambivalent: the valuable qualities of the Moors as middlemen, as experts in the pearl trade, and as soldiers were recognised, as well as their competitive position.

What of the effects of Dutch rule on the rise of caste divisions on a national or regional scale? The Karāva Catholics tended to be persecuted for their faith, and some were driven out into Kandyan territory, where they seem to have been tolerated according to traditional Buddhist principles. It has already been seen that some Karāva took to trading and carting in the King's domains, and rose in status and affluence in consequence. No doubt others grew rich in the Low Country. But the main effect of the Dutch in this field was undoubtedly on the caste that has become known as Salāgama (or cinnamon-peelers). The ancestors of this caste, who were originally called Chalias or Chaliyas, seems to have come as weavers from South India in comparatively recent times, and early observers placed them low in the hierarchy.[17] The Portuguese seem to have found the Salagama in coastal locations, and to have started their ascent of the social ladder by employing them in cinnamon peeling. It was the Dutch, however, who were mainly responsible for raising their status, for to the Dutch the cinnamon trade was the 'great industry', and cinnamon-peelers, though restricted in various ways (for example, they could not actually own land) were encouraged in others. Under Dutch tutelage they became highly-organised and self-conscious, and today they rank high in the hierarchy (under the Goyigama and Karāva as recognised even by Goyigama) and play a very important part in commerce and politics. They remain, however, Buddhists, and this is a commentary on the secular preoccupations of Dutch rule.

[17] Bryce Ryan, pp. 107–10.

Not that the Dutch were completely uninterested in religion. They persecuted Roman Catholics, as has been seen, and despised 'heathenism'. But they made few converts, and the Dutch Reformed Church survives in Ceylon virtually only amongst the Burghers.

Perhaps the greatest effect of Dutch rule was to complete the commercialisation of the Low-Country economy. Though this had few immediate effects on the ethnic and communal situation, apart from these just noted, Dutch activity nevertheless paved the way for British activity, which was fundamentally to affect the whole fabric of life in Ceylon in ways that have profoundly influenced the present communal position.

III. FOUR HUNDRED AND FIFTY YEARS OF FOREIGN RULE: THE BRITISH IN CEYLON

THE distinguished Ceylonese historian, Dr. G. C. Mendis, found himself able to declare 'The British period is undoubtedly the most important and the most interesting period of Ceylon History . . . During it Ceylon has gone through greater changes than in all its previous history'.[1] Mendis was, of course, thinking in general terms—of the transformation of a 'personal and feudal' form of government into one that is 'highly centralized and modern' and that has, moreover, undergone the further transmutation from colonial rule to responsible government; and of the tremendous economic and social changes during the period of British rule. But it may well be thought that Mendis' assertion is applicable also to the ethnic and communal situation. Not only did the British introduce new elements into the Ceylonese ethnic structure; but it was also during the British period that communal and caste tensions grew in force and that communal suspicions of a kind still all too familiar began to darken the scene—though, one hastens to add, not so much directly, through deliberate policy, as indirectly, through the revolutionary changes in the government, economy and society of Ceylon of which Mendis was thinking.

Given their Indian interests, it is not surprising that the British occasionally cast a glance towards Ceylon during Dutch times. In 1763, for example, with an eye to the excellence of the natural harbour at Trincomalee, they sought friendly relations with the King of Kandy. But it was not until 1795, mainly in order to deny Trincomalee

[1] G. C. Mendis, *Ceylon under the British*, 2nd ed. (Colombo, The Colombo Apothecaries, 1948), p. 6.

34 FOUR HUNDRED AND FIFTY YEARS OF FOREIGN RULE

and other harbours to the French during the wars, and in alliance with the Kings of Kandy, that the British took Trincomalee and, later that year and in the following year, other forts including that at Colombo itself. Dutch rule in the 'Maritime Provinces' was over, for after the war British suzerainty over these Provinces was confirmed. At first the newly occupied territory was governed by the British East India Company, but in 1802, after a violent rebellion of both Low-Country and Kandyan Sinhalese, Ceylon was placed directly under Britain as a Crown Colony, and so it remained until independence in 1948. The rebellion against Company rule had a communal element for, foolishly, the Company had brought in Madras Tamil civil officers to replace the local chieftains through whom both the Portuguese and the Dutch had ruled. These officers were followed by 'swarms of Tamils in the hope of farming the revenues'.[2] There were, however, other grievances over new taxes and the combination of revenue-collecting and judicial functions in one officer; but it is significant that the Committee which investigated the situation recommended 'the banishment of the Madrassis', as well as tax reform and the restoration of the authority of the Sinhalese chiefs.

From the first appearance of the British in Ceylon, certain Kandyan chiefs had been intriguing with them against their King, Sri Wickrama Rajasinha, a monarch of Tamil descent like his predecessor mentioned in the last chapter. To cut a long and confused story short, British forces entered Kandy on 14 February 1815, Sri Wickrama Rajasinha was deposed and exiled to Madras, and the Sinhalese kingdom came to an end. Because of the manner of its passing, the Kandyans are able to claim that their mountain fastness was never conquered but that, in the words of the Official Declaration of the Settlement of the Kandyan Provinces:

Led by the invitation of the chiefs, and welcomed by the acclamations of the people, the forces of His Britannic Majesty have entered the Kandyan territory, and penetrated to the capital. The

[2] H. W. Codrington, p. 159.

ruler of the interior provinces has fallen into their hands, and the government remains at the disposal of His Majesty's representative.[3]

On 2 March 1815 a Convention was held at Kandy between the British Governor and the Kandyan chiefs. At this, *inter alia*, the rights of the chiefs were guaranteed, and it was declared that the Buddhist religion, so vital a part of Sinhalese tradition, was to be maintained. The Kandyan system of administration through principal chiefs was retained, subject to the supervision of British Residents. Thus, for the time being at any rate, was the distinctiveness of the Kandyan kingdom preserved, even though 'the dynasty which had persisted in something less than a straight line for 2,300 years'[4] was at an end.

All was not yet to be at peace, however. A considerable rebellion broke out in the historic Uva Province (coterminous with the modern Badulla District, see Map 2) in 1817. It no doubt reflected a broad body of feeling among the Kandyan chiefs that the British, having ousted a tyrannical King, should withdraw again, Convention or no Convention, especially as there was clearly little sympathy among the British for the special position of Buddhism. But the spark that set Uva alight was struck on communal flint: the local Moors had been put by the British under their own headman, and great resentment was thus engendered. The British Resident, moreover, sent a party of Moors to arrest a Buddhist priest who had appeared in the jungle and who claimed to be a member of the royal family; and this did not help. The revolt spread like wildfire to other parts of the old kingdom, and but for jealousies among the Kandyan aristocracy (a long-term characteristic) might have succeeded. One result of the revolt was the devastation of the country, especially in Uva; another was that, the Convention having been broken, the administration of the

[3] Quoted by H. W. Codrington, p. 174.
[4] A. J. Tresidder, *Ceylon* (Princeton, Van Nostrand, 1960), p. 106.

country was placed directly under British officers, though Kandyan chiefs were retained as Disāvas of Provinces and as lesser headmen. Changes were also made in land tenure and in other spheres.

There were further though lesser disturbances Up-Country in 1820, 1823 and 1824; and the Government, learning from the Uva rebellion and from the later uprisings, that proper communications with the former Kandyan kingdom were essential, pressed on with a programme of road building. The road from Kurunegala to Kandy was opened in 1821, and the Colombo-Kandy road, through the Kadugannawa Pass, in 1825 (fulfilling an ancient prophecy that he who pierced the rock that blocked the Pass should receive the kingdom as a reward). Further roads were built in the ensuing years.

Already by 1825, then, a number of steps had been taken to assimilate the administration of the Kandyan territory to that of the rest of the country; and it might be expected that road construction would slowly lead to the erosion of Kandyan distinctiveness, even had no further measures been taken by the Government. But in the years after 1829 a commission of enquiry under W. M. G. Colebrooke and C. H. Cameron investigated the finances, administration and judicial system of Ceylon: the consequent Colebrooke-Cameron reforms, brought into force by an Order-in-Council on 28 September 1833, were thorough-going, even radical, in character and momentous in their results; and they form a striking exception to the generalisation that acts of British colonial policy tend to hallow or to sanction what has already happened in contrast to, say, Dutch or French policies with their tendency to apply the outcome of conscious reappraisals and to strike in new directions.

A word should perhaps be said in parenthesis about the principles which guided the authors of these reforms. G. C. Mendis has it that:

THE BRITISH IN CEYLON

Imbued with the ideas which brought about the Reform Act of 1832 in England and the abolition of the slave-trade, and influenced by writers like Adam Smith and Jeremy Bentham, Colebrooke and Cameron found much to criticize in the administration of Ceylon. They were convinced of the virtues of British conceptions of government, and believed ... that their institutions could be extended to the colonies ... they did not take a historical view of the question. They did not consider whether the people of Ceylon were advanced enough for the changes they contemplated or what the reactions to their proposals would be. They were out to modernize the Government of Ceylon and they made their proposals with that end in view.[5]

There seems no doubt that Cameron, a Scot and a barrister, was a Benthamite; but Colebrooke is at first sight a simple soldier, and soldiers are rarely political theorists, least of all radical ones.[6] But Colebrooke had served in Java when Sir Stamford Raffles was Lieutenant-Governor there, and had witnessed the abolition of the Dutch systems of forced cultivation and forced labour and the reform of the revenue system. Perhaps he saw in *rajakariya* (the performance of service to the king, or to his successors the British Government, in return for land tenure) a system of forced labour similar to that of the Dutch—which it was not—without understanding the consequences of its abolition; in other ways too he seems to have taken Raffles as his model without perfectly realising the relevance or otherwise of specific reforms to Ceylon conditions.

To return to the problem in question—the erosion of the distinctiveness of Kandyan territory—one immediate result of the Colebrooke–Cameron reforms was that separate administration of the Kandyan areas ceased, all Provinces throughout Ceylon being placed under British Government Agents. Disāvas, as chiefs over Provinces, were abolished, and the title, like that of Adigar (Minister) became an honour at the bestowal of the colonial Government. From

[5] G. C. Mendis, *Ceylon under the British*, p. 36.
[6] Cf. E. F. C. Ludowyk, pp. 166–69.

henceforth Kandyan chiefs ruled only as headmen over parts of Districts and over smaller divisions, though they retained picturesque traditional titles (Ratemahatmaya, Korāle and so on). This deposition from high office, with other reforms obnoxious to the chiefs, led to an unsuccessful conspiracy in 1834.

History during Portuguese and Dutch times, it has been seen, created and then widened the gap between Low-Country and Kandyan Sinhalese. But by 1911 E. B. Denham was able to write:

The distinction between Kandyans and Low-Country Sinhalese is every year lessened; in fact one of the most conspicuous features of the decade has been the amalgamation which is steadily taking place of Low-Country and Kandyan Sinhalese. It would be strange if this were not so in modern times, when improved means of communication bring the villager from even the remotest part of the Island in touch with town life.[7]

There must undoubtedly have been a great deal of truth in this. But some of the distinctiveness of Kandyan territory remained when I first knew it eighteen years ago, and remains today: this is particularly true of Kandyan villages in the remoter parts of the lowland Dry Zone. For, in spite of a broadly uniform system of administration throughout the country, government action in British times continued to recognise the special case of Kandyan territory in a number of ways (for example, in the application of laws of inheritance, marriage and divorce, and in certain enactments concerning land); and, much more important from the point of view of this booklet, Kandyan territory Up-Country was affected by the development of plantations to a greater degree than Low-Country or Tamil districts, not least in terms of ethnic composition and communal tension.

Plantations were not new in the Ceylon of the mid-nineteenth century. The Dutch had planted cinnamon

[7] E. B. Denham, p. 213.

(hence 'Cinnamon Gardens', the most exclusive residential district of Colombo) and coconut, among other crops. The British early on retained the monopoly of cinnamon which they had inherited from the Dutch and tried, without very much success at first, to stimulate the Sinhalese to open new plantations of this and other commercial crops; later they took to coconuts with more enthusiasm. After the removal of restrictions which the East India Company had placed on planting by Europeans outside Colombo, many Englishmen and others opened up land in the Low Country in coffee, cotton, sugar, indigo and opium; and, after 1815, coffee cultivation especially spread to the Kandyan hill country, where Sinhalese as well as Europeans began to engage in it. There were also government plantations, worked by *rajakariya*. The building of the roads to Kandy greatly benefited this extension of coffee planting.

But plantation agriculture did not really get under way until after 1835, when the operation of a number of factors conspired in its favour; these included the lowering of the rate for the import of coffee from Ceylon into the United Kingdom, to the same as that applicable to West Indian coffee (which had previously enjoyed a preference). The Government made Crown Land readily available, free of land tax (as recommended by Colebrooke and Cameron); and in 1840 enacted the Crown Lands Encroachments Ordinance, under which land considered 'waste' was declared Crown property. A great upsurge of coffee production took place:[8] exports rose from 20,911 cwt. per annum (the average from 1828 to 35) to nearly 200,000 cwt. in 1845. A greats peculative coffee boom set in, and in spite of slumps from time to time (there was one in 1845–7) the area under coffee continued to grow, Sinhalese, as well as Europeans and others engaging in planting.

---

[8] For an imaginative account of the pioneer phase in coffee planting in Up-country Ceylon, see Christine Wilson's novel *The Bitter Berry*, (London, Hurst and Blackett, 1957).
[9] G. C. Mendis, *Ceylon under the British*, pp. 45–6.

Exports reached 856,570 cwt. in 1875. But the coffee plantations were then smitten by a terrible fungus disease, the notorious *Hemeleia vastatrix*. In due course, however, much land that had been planted Up-Country in coffee came to be planted in tea, which also extended into new land. Rubber came to occupy a great deal of land at lower elevations, in the Low Country proper and on the lower slopes of the Kandyan hills; and coconut planting (though this was mainly in small-holdings) spread north of Colombo, fanning out to occupy much land in the triangle between Chilaw, Kurunegala and the capital.

Some early European plantations had used local labour (under *rajakariya* in the case of government estates) but by the time that coffee began to boom labour supply had become a real problem. As Mendis says:

The abolition of *rajakariya* did not solve the labour problem on the plantations. Many people expected that once people were released from their services to Government, and were allowed to choose any occupations they desired, the plantations would get the labour they needed. But this did not happen. Every Sinhalese was attached to his village. Both by custom and by Roman-Dutch law he was entitled to a share of the property of his parents. When *rajakariya* was abolished he tended his own lands, and did not show any desire to migrate from his village and work in the coffee plantations. Moreover, if he was of 'high' caste, he considered it beneath his dignity to become a paid labourer. Thus the planters did not get enough labour to work their plantations. Sinhalese from the lowlands came and served as carpenters and masons. Villagers took part in destroying forests and opening up land. But only a section of those who lived close to the plantations came for regular work as labourers.'[10]

The solution was to import labour from south India, a step that was to prove momentous in its consequences not only for the economic development of Ceylon but also in terms of communal relations. As early as 1828 Sir Edward Barnes,

[10] G. C. Mendis, *Ceylon under the British*, p. 47.

Governor of Ceylon from 1824–31 (who was keenly interested in coffee cultivation) and George Bird (who had opened the first European coffee plantation at Sinhapitiya, near Gampola, in 1823), recruited 150 labourers from south India; but they nearly all deserted within a year.[11] But the main stream of immigration came later, with and after the great coffee boom: between 1843 and 1859 no fewer than 903,557 men, women and children came to work on the new plantations;[12] others came in due course, to work as labourers on railways and roads, in the harbours, and as scavengers and unskilled labourers generally; but the plantations, first of coffee, then of tea and rubber, have been the main absorbent of Indian labour, nearly all of it Tamil.

How, it may be asked, was this enormous labour force recruited? It appears that early on the planters tried to persuade the Ceylon Government to act as its recruiting agent; but that the Colonial Office, true to *laissez faire* principles, was not willing that it should take on the task,[13] though the transport was subsidised. Accordingly a vast private system was set up, under which *kanganies* (foremen) recruited labour in the villages of Tamil Nad, paying advances as a cash inducement to migrate. These advances, together with the cost of the passage and other expenses, were later deducted from the labourers' pay, and until 1921 the labourer was not free to leave the plantation until his debt was discharged. Many *kanganies* made a great deal of money, partly by acting as moneylenders, but the fact that the labourer was willing to migrate when all the financial dice seemed loaded against him is an indication of the poverty of south India, which was clearly such that Ceylon was seen as a land of plenty in spite of the hazards of the journey. These hazards were, to begin with, daunting enough, and the immigrant Tamils died in their thousands

[11] G. C. Mendis, p. 35.
[12] E. F. C. Ludowyk, p. 196.
[13] *Ibid.*, p. 195.

as they made their way through the malarial jungles of the Dry Zone on their way to the Kandyan highlands. There, too, death overtook many more of them, for medical care—if it existed at all—was at best rudimentary. During the 1840s the death rate amongst Up-Country labourers was put at 250 per thousand.[14] Only gradually did labour legislation, improved sanitation and medical care begin to alleviate matters. Yet, all along, labourers who survived managed to save money and to remit it to India, or to take it back with them when they returned to their home villages: for many Tamil labourers were, for a long time, birds of passage, who had no desire to settle permanently in Ceylon. Only comparatively recently has this trend been reversed.

What was the effect on the ethnic and communal situation in Ceylon of the Indian Tamil labourers who thus arrived there with so much difficulty and hardship? By 1911, when Ceylon and Indian Tamils were first separated in the census returns, there were already more Indian than Ceylon Tamils: 530,983 of the former compared with 528,024 of the latter. The impact of this large new element in the ethnic composition of Ceylon has been all the greater because it has been so heavily concentrated geographically. In 1953, Indian Tamils formed 20 per cent or more of the total population in Kandy, Matale, Nuwara Eliya, Badulla Ratnapura and Mannar Districts (see Map 2 p. 60). Mannar District is, of course, on the north-west coast of the lowland Dry Zone, and Indians form a high proportion of its small population (43,711 in 1953) because of proximity to Tamil Nad rather than because of the presence of estates. All the other Districts named are in the Kandyan parts of the central highlands, and in all but one of them (Ratnapura District) the relatively high proportion of Indians is associated with tea estates. In Ratnapura District rubber is the principal estate crop.

It can be seen immediately, then, that it is on the Kandyan Sinhalese that the Indian Tamils mainly impinge, and it is

[14] E. F. C. Ludowyk, p. 196.

not surprising that it is mainly from the Kandyan Sinhalese that the reaction has come. In much of Kandy, Matale and Badulla Districts, and more recently in large parts of the rubber lands in Ratnapura District, the land that was alienated to planters was mainly the scrub and jungle that lay on the higher slopes of the valleys in which lay the ancient villages of the Kandyans. The Kandyans cultivated their rice in the valley bottoms or in terraces skilfully and laboriously constructed on the lower slopes, and nearby lay their village gardens in which grew coconuts, areca nuts and others tree and vegetable crops. The upper slopes, the terrain taken for plantations, was used in former times for grazing, for hunting, as a source of timber, and for shifting cultivation; or, if population expanded, as a reserve of land on to which paddy fields or gardens might be extended. There has been much argument as to whether or not the Crown was exerting rights over this land that had been exercised by the Sinhalese kings.[15] Whatever the rights or wrongs of this controversy, the fact is that Kandyan villages have been effectively hemmed in by the estates, as is easy to demonstrate in the field, and that population expansion, and the spread of cash crops, during the British period has forced them to use up almost all of the useful land outside the estates and, more recently, led to acute land hunger. Not surprisingly, the Kandyan villager and Kandyan politician, unable or unwilling to recognise the benefits that the estates have brought to the economy of the island, see only, or profess to see only that they have been part of a process that has imposed landlessness and poverty on the villager and forced him latterly to do what he would never do 100 years ago—to work regularly as an estate labourer.

The estates too, especially the tea estates of the hills, have functioned so distinctly from the old villages that for a long

---

[15] Cf. for example, *Report of the Kandyan Peasantry Commission*, Ceylon Sessional Paper No. 18 of 1951 (Colombo, Govt. Press, 1951), pp. 71–4.

time the economy of the region was a classic instance of a dual economy. On the one hand there were the ancient villages, owned and worked by Sinhalese, most of their produce being consumed locally. On the other hand, there were the estates, owned by Europeans or, later, European companies, worked by Indian Tamil labour, and producing almost entirely for export. To begin with the two sides of the economy, the one in the valley-bottoms, the other on the hill-tops, were almost as separate as oil and water in a jar; except that Sinhalese labour played some part in clearing jungle and in building and similar operations. Gradually the boundary has become blurred. Estates have come to be owned more and more by Ceylonese (though by no means exclusively by Kandyans); latterly, as has been seen, local Sinhalese have had to take to work on estates. The villagers have increasingly turned to cash crops, especially to those they have seen successfully grown on local estates. But if the economy, though retaining some of the marks of duality, is becoming more unified, the society still remains plural: the Indian Tamil remains separate from the Kandyan Sinhalese, retaining his language and his Hindu religion, marrying only his own kind, to a very large extent living his life on his hillsides and hill-tops as though the Kandyans were not there at all (though in places one hears complaints that Indian Tamils, especially *Kanganies*, act as village moneylenders and in course of time acquire village land, either by foreclosing on mortgages or by purchase).[16]

Or, to put this important matter another way round, the Sinhalese social system had found itself able in the past to absorb immigrants from South India who settled down in its midst: it has been seen that probably both the Karāva and Salāgama had a history of this sort. The Sinhalese had adopted the classic Indian solution to the

[16] Cf. for example, *Report of the Kandyan Peasantry Commission*, p. 275, for complaints of this nature in Pata Hewaheta, a hilly area south-east of Kandy town.

intrusion of an alien group—it made the alien group into a new caste or sub-caste, and converted it to the religion of the majority. Perhaps we can regard the Portuguese Burghers as a group in transit to the same destination. But the Indian Tamil estate labourers poured in much too fast for absorption, and in many smaller parts of Kandyan territory they became the majority community. Moreover, their location and their work isolated them from the Kandyan Sinhalese. So an alien group they remained, and against them in time there came to be directed much of the frustrated hostility which the Kandyan Sinhalese came to feel for the estate system in general.

The impact of the Indian Tamil came quite differently, however, in other parts of the hill area, especially in the plateaux and valleys above 2,000 feet in the Nuwara Eliya District and in adjacent parts of Kandy and Badulla District. Here the pioneer planters found square mile after square mile of virgin forest, with no significant Sinhalese settlement at all. Here there was no question of a dual economy, or of the cribbing of the Sinhalese village in its narrow valley. Rather there developed a great area of monoculture, first of coffee and then of tea, with a population almost entirely Indian Tamil, except for European planters and supervisors, railway workers, government servants, and so on. In Nuwara Eliya District in 1953, 59 per cent of the population was Indian Tamil in spite of the fact that the northern part of the District includes lower land in which there are Kandyan Sinhalese villages. In Kotmale Division of the same District, 119,268 out of 163,115 inhabitants were Indians; while in the adjacent Uda Bulathgama Division of Kandy District the proportion was 126,421 to 167,740. Here, then, are large, solid, bodies of Indian Tamils, even less likely to be absorbed in the classic way than their compatriots at lower levels: less likely, it is true, to excite by their own presence the hostility of a Kandyan Sinhalese villager who sees his village hemmed in by estates, but nevertheless liable to be affected by the feeling against Indian Tamils engendered in the Kandyan valleys.

The opening up of the Kandyan hill areas to commerce and to plantations had the further effect of producing new urban settlements with a very mixed population. It has already been seen that Low-Country Sinhalese found employment in the later days of the Kandyan kingdom as carters and on early estates in similar work and as builders. There came as time went on a very considerable influx of Low-Country Sinhalese, particularly into towns like Kandy, Matale and Nuwara Eliya; all of these had between one-quarter and one-third of their population made up of Low-Country Sinhalese in 1953, while in Kandy and Nuwara Eliya Low-Country outnumbered Kandyan Sinhalese. There was also a movement of Ceylon Tamils, Ceylon and Indian Moors and others into these formerly Kandyan areas.

One of the outstanding effects of economic development during the British period in Ceylon was thus a revolutionary change in the ethnic composition of the former fastness of the Kandyan Sinhalese, to produce the result summed up in Map 2. In other parts of Ceylon, apart from some areas of the Low Country affected by rubber planting, ethnic changes were by comparison slight. It is easy to see from Map 2 that Colombo, Kalutara, Galle, Matara and Hambantota Districts have their expected large majorities of Low-Country Sinhalese, while Jaffna and Vavuniya have correspondingly large Ceylon Tamil majorities. The mixed nature of the population in Mannar District and in Batticaloa and Trincomalee Districts has already been commented upon; and in Kegalla and Kurunegala Districts, in spite of planting, 72 per cent and 74 per cent respectively of the population in 1953 were Kandyan Sinhalese. But the real stronghold of the Kandyans became Anuradhapura District and other similar parts of the lowland Dry Zone; 72 per cent of the population of Anuradhapura District in 1911 were Kandyans (the figure had been reduced to 66 per cent in 1953 because of recent colonisation). The point here is, of course, that coffee, tea and rubber will not grow under lowland Dry Zone conditions: coconut will only grow where a high water-table is preserved round its roots, and in the nineteenth century merely spread in a limited way to such areas as the Jaffna peninsula, Mannar Island, and the Puttalam and Batticaloa coasts. Accordingly, there was virtually no development of plantation agriculture, or of small-holder cultivation of commercial crops, in the Dry Zone during the British period. Moreover, the whole Zone was heavily malarial, and there was little settlement by peasant or others from other parts of the island.[17] If the Kandyan region as a whole had been isolated from the effects of Portuguese and Dutch rule, the lowland Dry Zone was for the most part preserved from the major effects of British rule; and its isolation meant not only comparative freedom from alien immigration but the survival of a social order that was under attack elsewhere.

But if, outside the Kandyan hills, the ethnic effects of British rule were relatively slight, nevertheless in most areas the result was a more mixed population than would be shown if it were possible to produce a version of Map 2 for, say, 1795 or 1815. This in itself may well indicate a predisposition to communal tension. If the population of an area is of uniform community and religion, no local incident or frustration can spark off communal trouble though, of course, if the community concerned is in a minority nationally it may feel frustrated on national issues. But a mixed population of the sort produced in many areas during British rule is more likely to find occasion for division on communal lines.

For most of the British period, however, from the Uva rebellion until the coming of independence, there was

[17] Cf. B. H. Farmer, *Pioneer Peasant Colonization in Ceylon* (London, Oxford University Press for Royal Institute of International Affairs, 1957), pp. 102–139.

little overt communal trouble, with the exception of certain incidents and trends to be noted in a moment. The country was at peace under the *Pax Britannica*, and population and export figures bore witness to the effects of British rule. In some ways at least it was caste tension rather than communal tension that became most evident as British rule wore on. This may appear a curious situation to those who imagine that caste withers away under the blaze of egalitarianism introduced from the West; but the facts in Ceylon were otherwise.

It will be remembered that by the beginning of British times some members of the once-lowly Karāva and Salāgama castes had become wealthy and influential owing to their participation in commerce. The upward trend in the fortunes of these people continued in British times, and more of their caste-fellows joined them. Some of them started as carters and became contractors, others pursued commerce with singular success, others took to planting. One of the earliest coffee planters, for example, was Joronis de Soysa of Moratuwa, who planted over 1,000 acres at Hanguranketa, near Kandy, with money earned by selling arrack.[18] He employed as managers men from his own village, often relatives, and thus characteristically demonstrated caste solidarity. Other members of the family (which still owns the property) started the first bank in Ceylon and were to their credit generous philanthropists. Other Low-Countrymen took a lion's share of the task of opening up the Colombo–Chilaw–Kurenegala triangle for coconut planting; here the name of Sir Henry de Mel stands out. Still others invested in the rubber-planting industry when that in its turn came to Ceylon.

As can well be imagined, the reaction of the Goyigama, and especially of the Kandyan aristocracy, to the intrusion into land-owning of these Low-Countrymen was rather that of the English aristocrat of ancient lineage to the intrusion

[18] E. F. C. Ludowyk, p. 202.

of a *nouveau riche* industrialist into his ancestral countryside (though it should be added that many Goyigama were not slow to plant wide acres in the new crops themselves). But whereas the English parvenu is traditionally at pains to have himself, or at least his sons and daughters, assimilated to the land-owning aristocracy, so that in a generation or two the old and the new are not readily distinguishable, the reaction of the wealthy Karāva, Salāgama and others was very different. They maintained their caste solidarity, and kept their wealth within the caste by arranging suitable matches for their sons and daughters. They may have concealed caste by adopting or perpetuating Portuguese names, but they did not try to assimilate themselves to the Goyigama—an overture of that sort would in any case have met with a very dusty answer. Nor did they absorb Western social ideas and seek to destroy the caste system—at least, they were inconsistent and ambivalent if they did occasionally pay lip service to the idea of social equality. Rather did they seek to prove that their own caste was as good as, if not better than, the Goyigama. The Karāva concerned, for example, were at pains to 'show' from elaborate genealogies that they were really Ksshatriya, warriors according to the Indian system (and thus superior to the Goyigama), who, perhaps, came to Ceylon as trusted captains for the Portuguese. Similar aggressive claims were made on behalf of other Low-Country castes.

As Bryce Ryan has pointed out, towards the end of the nineteenth century and until 1925 or so, some of the bitterest fulminations in Ceylon were not inter-communal, but inter-caste.[19] The non-Goyigama castes, especially those just named, sought to establish their own high place in the hierarchy and to establish that the Goyigama were usurpers or worse. The Goyigama retaliated. The battle was carried on with a vigour and a degree of vituperation that has few parallels except in the bitterest of communal

[19] Bryce Ryan, pp. 332–5.

encounters of recent years: yet it has found few echoes in the West because most of the attack is written in Sinhalese. The scars of the battle have by no means healed, and caste remains a potent force in Ceylon politics to this day.

The verbal duel between the Karāva and the Goyigama was made all the more bitter because so many of the Karāva involved were Christians, while most of the Goyigama had remained faithful to Buddhism; and because Buddhism had, after decades of comparative stagnation, began to show signs of life once again. To this religious situation the British contributed their quota, though they had nothing like the startling impact of their Portuguese forerunners. Figures for the number of Christians in Ceylon in early British days are unbelievably high because many Ceylonese thought of Christianity as the 'government religion' which they were bound by regulation to adopt for official purposes, whatever their convictions.[20] The British certainly gave the impression, early on at any rate, that 'conversion' to Christianity, especially to Protestantism, was a mark in a man's favour. Whether for this reason, or from genuine conviction, a number of families became Anglican, particularly among the Karāva, but also among aristocratic Kandyan families and in Jaffna, while the Wesleyans had some success in Colombo, Galle, Kandy and Batticaloa; American Congregationalists were active in Jaffna. But during British times Roman Catholicism continued to advance, and more than maintained its preponderance as the dominant Christian sect. When Denham was writing in 1911 the Christians in Ceylon were made up of 339,300 Roman Catholics, 41,095 Anglicans, 3,546 Presbyterians, 17,323 Wesleyans, 3,306 Baptists, 2,978 Congregationalists and 1,620 others.

But the educational work of the Christian missions was in many ways more important than their strictly missionary endeavour. For it was the missionary societies who, in

[20] E. B. Denham, p. 266.

addition to other educational work, pioneered secondary education in English. Until the 1880s, all but one of Ceylon's secondary schools were missionary foundations, and all taught in English. The curriculum of these schools had many limitations;[21] but their great memorial was the production of an English-speaking élite, drawn from all the principal communities of the country and from all those castes which had inherited or acquired affluence; an élite familiar with the social and political thinking of the West (and in particular of Britain) and in many ways the most English of Asians and more English than the English— the 'Brown Sahibs' of Tarzie Vittachi's recent amusing, but nevertheless percipient, little book.[22] It was this élite that was to build a new caste, as it were, (though divided into 'sub-castes' according to the older caste divisions within it) severed from all other groups in the country by its English speech and education; and that was to form not only the spearhead of the nationalist movement but also to fill the Civil Service and the other branches of government. The tensions between this group and the nation at large (or at least articulate parts of it) have been a strong influence in recent politics.

Now the possibilities for secondary education, and with it the provenance of this new élite, were very unevenly distributed over the island. Provision was relatively lavish in the Low Country, especially in Colombo, and here there grew up that inter-community, inter-caste élite whose Englishness made them so ill-informed about the country at large and whose apparent lack of communal and caste feeling, combined with their divorce from the majority of the people, was to deceive many a foreign observer about the true dynamics of affairs in Ceylon.

Mission schools were thick on the ground in Jaffna and to this, together with habits of seriousness and industry, is to be attributed the success of the Jaffna Tamils in entering

[21] See E. F. C. Ludowyk, pp. 215–20.
[22] Tarzie Vittachi, *The Brown Sahib* (London, André Deutsch, 1962).

government service in numbers disproportionate to their strength in the country (though not to the extent often made out). Ceylon Tamils from Jaffna began, as the nineteenth century wore on, to move south to jobs in Colombo and elsewhere, adding to the ethnic variety of the towns and to the possibilities of communal tension and disharmony. The Burghers (or some of them) also benefited disproportionately by English-style education. In early British days they tended to dominate the clerical service, though they later lost ground.

It was as a reaction to missionary activity, too, that there came the Buddhist and Hindu revival of the late nineteenth century, which gathered force in the twentieth. Buddhism, it will be remembered, underwent something of a revival in the later days of the Kandyan kingdom, and this had some effect in the Low Country too in the early decades of the nineteenth century. By about 1860 a group of Buddhist priests, concluding that the traditional passivity of their religion could not be maintained in the face of Christian mission activity, began counter-missionary work. Buddhist vernacular schools were established, while in 1880 the Buddhist Theosophical Society was founded in order to establish further Buddhist schools, one of which became the present Ananda College, one of Colombo's leading secondary schools. The Buddhist revival also took other forms: public controversy with Christians, a revival of interest in ancient language and literature. There were similar developments in the north. Societies were formed by members of the élite who had retained their Hinduism, papers and pamphlets poured forth, and in due course Jaffna Hindu College was founded.

These developments were important. For both Sinhalese and Tamils they formed part of a reaction from complete submission to Westernisation and hence an important ingredient in the movement towards nationalism and national independence. From the communal point of view, they served to perpetuate differences between Sinhalese and

Tamil, between Buddhist and Hindu; and, so far as Buddhism is concerned, identified Buddhism with the national revival. In the last few years we have witnessed what could be brought about by a Buddhist revival with these associations when it was at last in full flood.

But what, it may be said, of constitutional advance, that hallmark of British imperialism, in its relation to communal problems? This has purposely been left until last because in many ways it reflects the position created by the other factors discussed in this Chapter; though, of course, it has been held to have exaggerated the tensions produced by those factors.

As early as 1833, a Legislative Council was established in Ceylon, and there were to be nominated Ceylonese members *ab initio*; but no Ceylonese acquainted with English (as was essential) was willing to serve. In 1835, however, a Sinhalese and a Tamil who were government interpreters were nominated, with a Burgher. Thus early did a form of communal representation begin. Throughout the peaceful later nineteenth century, however, the Legislative Council was little more than a sounding board for the Executive, which consisted entirely of officials.

Agitation for the reform of the legislature came at first almost entirely from European interests and from the Burghers, who together formed the Ceylon League in 1865 to press for constitutional change. Later the new middle-class élite joined in the agitation and, significantly, pressed for elected representation on a non-communal basis (except for the reservation of a few seats for minorities like Burghers and Muslims).

It was not until 1912 that the reformed Council came into being. An official majority was maintained, but the rural Europeans, the urban Europeans, the Burghers and the 'educated Ceylonese' (that is, the English-educated) each elected one member, while six nominated members represented Low-Country Sinhalese (2), Kandyan Sinhalese (1), Tamils (2) and Muslims (1). One of the nominated Low-

Country Sinhalese seats went to a non-Goyigama and one of the Tamil seats to a non-Vellāla. The 'educated' Ceylonese, again significantly, chose a Ceylon Tamil, Sir Ponnambalam Ramanathan, as their first member.

It is interesting, in retrospect, that communal wrangling over representation goes back to the moves that led up to these changes. Thus the second Tamil-nominated member was added as a result of Tamil claims that they would otherwise be under-represented. Although one does not wish to accuse the British Government or its agents of deliberately dividing so that it might rule, one cannot but agree with Mendis' judgement:

> On the whole the reforms helped to perpetuate the divisions in society, the special interests of which the British system of administration for over a century has tended to obliterate. Though the Educated Ceylonese electorate brought together the English-educated classes among the Sinhalese, the Tamils and the Muslims, the grant of separate electorates to the Europeans and the Burghers helped these communities to consider themselves as separate entities rather than as citizens of Ceylon.[23]

Meanwhile, the élite, dissatisfied with the 1912 reforms, found their campaign for further change reinforced from an unexpected quarter—the outcome of the first communal rioting for a long time. This broke out in 1915 as a result of an affair in Gampola, where a group of Indian Moors objected to a Buddhist procession passing their mosque. The Indian Moors, in turn, were resented as arrogant intruders, very different from the old-established Ceylon Moors. As so often happens, one incident led to another until trouble spread to Kandy and Moor shops were looted. It seems that British officials greatly exaggerated the nature of the riots and, fearing a plot against the state in time of war, arrested a number of 'educated Ceylonese', including D. S. Senanayake, who was later to be Ceylon's first Prime Minister. These leaders were prominent in a

[23] G. C. Mendis, p. 122.

Buddhist temperance movement which had popular backing, and the arrests led to a wave of mass feeling for nationalism, which had earlier been not much more than a movement among the élite.

Political leadership however, stayed with the élite, and the spearhead which eventually broke through to responsible government typifies its throughly mixed nature: it was formed by Sir Ponnambalam Arunachalam, a Ceylon Tamil and Hindu; Sir James Peiris, a Karāva Sinhalese and an Anglican; and by Sinhalese Goyigama Buddhists like Senanayake and D. B. Jayatilaka. Men like this were prominent in the Ceylon National Congress, formed in 1919 and in close contact with Indian Nationalism.

In 1921 reform of the Legislative Council was announced. Elected members were in a stronger position, but were still in a minority. The principle of communal representation was perpetuated, and the one non-communal seat, that for an elected 'educated Ceylonese', was suppressed. Additional nominated seats were created, one for the Kandyans, one for the Indians, together with three for 'special interests'. Two such interests, the Chamber of Commerce and the Low-Country Products Association, received an elected member each, while the Low-Country Sinhalese and Tamils were given eleven members between them on a territorial basis. The Congress condemned the new arrangement for introducing 'invidious distinctions between communities', for creating special interests, and for excluding the Kandyans from the territorial electorates. A little later the Ceylon Tamils left the Congress because in the event they found themselves with only three members while the Low-Country Sinhalese had eleven and the Kandyans two. They demanded two-thirds of the number of seats given to the Sinhalese, and refused to be won back by the Congress leaders. Setting the pattern for many later occasions, proposals and counter-proposals for further reform were made, the Congress never departing from the principle of territorial electorates, though willing to include special representatives for minorities, the Tamils and others making alternative proposals on communal lines.[24]

The basic dilemma that confronts representative government in a country riven by communal differences is here plain for all to see: territorial electorates, drawn with no eye to the distribution of communities, mean rule by the majority community with no safeguard for the minorities, while safeguards for the minorities inevitably deepen the divisions of the nation on communal lines.

Subsequent wrangling about constitutional development undoubtedly heightened communal feeling and quickened the apprehension of the minorities. In 1923 a further measure of reform increased the weight of elected membership without giving an elected majority, but still maintained provision for communal representation. In 1931 a Commission headed by Lord Donoughmore visited Ceylon and produced a scheme for more radical constitutional change.[25] The commissioners were made all too well aware of the communal dissension and distrust that by now darkened the political scene in Ceylon and with the strength of communal, rather than national feeling. They came to the conclusion, however, that communal representation must be abolished, not least because of the suspicion and animosity they believed it had bred. They therefore recommended territorial electorates, to the number of sixty-five, but with provision for twelve nominated members to speak for minority interests otherwise unrepresented. (The Secretary of State reduced these to fifty and eight respectively, and introduced universal adult suffrage). They further concluded that a parliamentary system on British lines would but sharpen communal divisions, and so recommended the creation of a State Council to have both legislative and executive functions and to split into Executive Committees,

[24] For details, cf. G. C. Mendis, p. 126 and W. Howard Wriggins, *Ceylon: the Dilemmas of a New Nation* (Princeton, N.J., Princeton University Press, 1960), pp. 80–90.
[25] *Ceylon: Report of the Special Commission on the Constitution* (Donoughmore Report), (London, H.M.S.O., Cmd. 3131, 1928).

one for each subject (agriculture, transport and so on) under the chairmanship of a Minister.[26] There would thus be no chance for parties to form on communal lines, with minorities in perpetual opposition. In fact, however, the Cabinet was all-Sinhalese from 1936 until 1942; and the Tamils were strongly against the whole arrangement. For reasons that need not detain us here, the Donoughmore constitution was also strongly attacked from almost all other quarters as well.

In 1944–45 a further constitutional Commission, this time under the leadership of Lord Soulbury, visited Ceylon and considered what constitutional changes should be made in the light of the working of the Donoughmore constitution and of the promise made by the British Government that Ceylon should move towards 'full, responsible government under the Crown'.[27] A number of electoral schemes designed to deal with the communal problem were presented to Lord Soulbury and his colleagues, among them the 'fifty-fifty' proposal—that the Sinhalese should receive half of the seats, and all the minorities together, including the Indian Tamils, the other half. By this time, the Ceylon Tamils, whose leaders favoured this scheme, were organised in the All-Ceylon Tamil Congress. In the event the commissioners favoured territorial representation, but with a formula for the delimitation of constituencies which was weighted to take account of area as well as population and thus favoured the Ceylon Moor and Tamil minorities living in scattered villages in the Dry Zone (though hardly the compact mass of Tamils in Jaffna). These proposals formed part of the new constitution which became effective in May 1946 and brought, in effect, parliamentary government on the Westminster model, and so became part of the constitutional machinery of independent Ceylon on 4 February 1948.

[26] For an excellent critique of this and other aspects of the Donoughmore constitution cf. W. Howard Wriggins, pp. 85–90.
[27] *Ceylon: Report of the Commission on Constitutional Reform* (Soulbury Report) (London, H.M.S.O., Cmd. 6677, 1945).

It will be seen, then, that the conventional view that Ceylon made a peaceful transition from colonial status to independence is in large measure justified. Apart from the 1915 riots (which were hardly part of the movement towards independence) there were no disturbances, no violence, not even civil disobedience. No leaders, apart from those arrested (apparently by mistake) in 1915 suffered imprisonment; relations between Ceylonese leaders and the colonial power remained excellent. But it will also be seen that it is wrong to assume that because the first few years of independence were peaceful the communal problem had been solved. This Chapter should have created an impression of lowering skies—with the arrival of the Indian Tamils, the gathering caste and religious dissensions around the turn of the century, and the wrangles between communities over constitutional reform as the main clouds spreading over the horizon. All of these clouds and more were to bring heavy and indeed disastrous storms during the first decade of independence.

IV. CEYLON SINCE INDEPENDENCE

DURING the first eight years of Ceylon's independence (1948–56) the United National Party dominated the political scene. It is significant that the party has an English name and that though it now has a Sinhalese title ('Eksath Jatika Paksha') it has always been the 'U.N.P.' (in English) even to politicians making speeches in Sinhalese. For the U.N.P. was essentially a party of the élite whose evolution was described in the last Chapter. Founded by D. S. Senanayake in 1945–46, it brought together his Sinhalese associates from the old State Council and from the Ceylon National Congress, the Ceylon Muslim League, a number of Ceylon Tamils and, at the outset, S.W.R.D. Bandaranaike's 'Sinhala Maha Sabha' (again significantly, a party with a Sinhalese name meaning 'Great Sinhalese Party'). D. S. Senanayake undoubtedly had constantly before him the vision of a United Ceylon; and in 1948 even the leader of the Tamil Congress, G. G. Ponnambalam, joined his party. All the political leaders in the U.N.P. were Western-educated and upper middle-class, and most of them were Goyigama, though they could count on the support of wealthy Karāva, largely because they were anti-Left. Indeed, the Left was one of the only two significant political elements to be excluded from the U.N.P. The other was the Indian Tamil group, and thereby hangs the tale of what, on the surface, was the only communal storm in those peaceable days of U.N.P. rule.

Under the Donoughmore constitution Indian Tamils and other Indians who could prove that they were domiciled or permanently resident in Ceylon were enfranchised. The number thus entitled to vote had risen to 225,000 by 1939,[1] and certain Up-Country constituencies tended to return Indian Tamil members on a communal ticket. There was

[1] E. F. C. Ludowyk, p. 259.

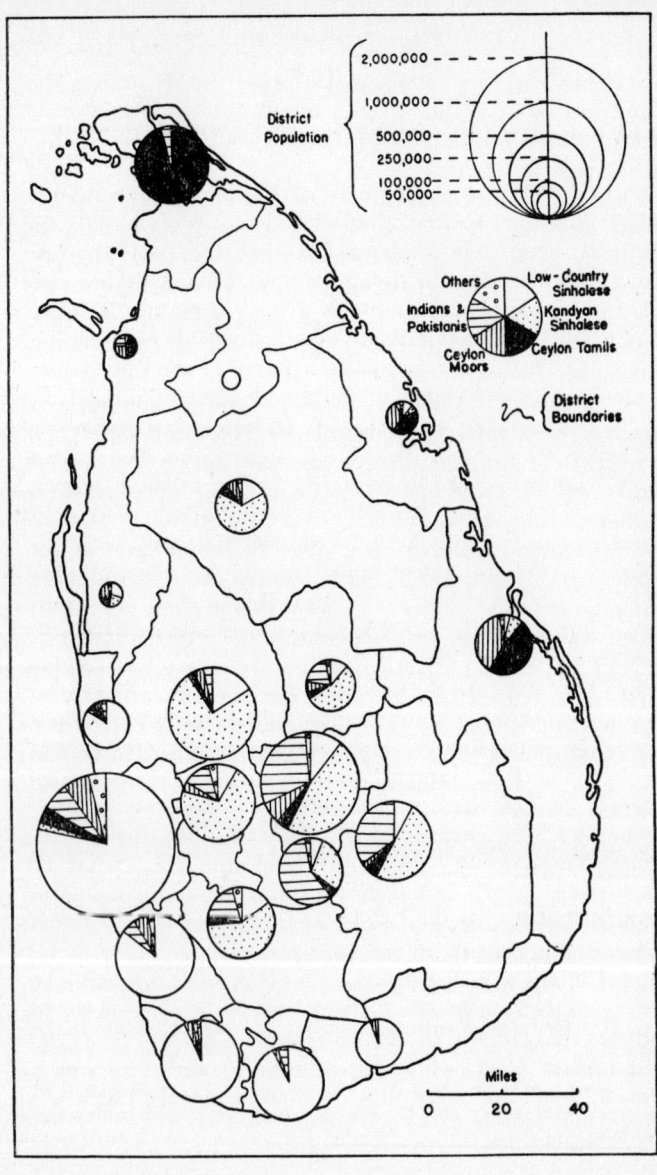

considerable feeling on this matter, particularly among the Kandyans, and, as has been pointed out by W. Howard Wriggins, more hours have been spent in the Ceylon Parliament on this than on any other single subject.[2] With the coming of independence, the U.N.P. Government set about limiting the political rights of Indians in Ceylon, primarily by enacting the Citizenship Act No. 18 of 1948, which limits Ceylon citizenship to those who can claim it by descent (this effectively included only Sinhalese, Ceylon Tamils and other long-resident groups) or by registration. Citizenship by registration was available to those intending to be 'ordinarily resident in Ceylon'; and the Indian and Pakistan Residents (Citizenship) Act No. 3 of 1949 then proceeded to provide that a claimant for registration of Indian or Pakistani descent had to have been resident continuously since 1 January 1946 and to have been in residence before that for ten years (if unmarried) or for seven years (if married). Documentary proof of residence was required. The effect of this legislation has been that which was intended—to limit very severely the number of Indians, especially Indian Tamils, able to claim Ceylon citizenship. And since the Ceylon (Parliamentary Elections) Amendment Act No. 48 of 1949 provided that only a citizen of Ceylon should be enfranchised, large numbers of Indian Tamils were disenfranchised, and remain so. Only about 100,000 of them have in fact been registered as citizens.

[2] W. Howard Wriggins, p. 212. Wriggins has an excellent account of the recent state of the Indian question, pp. 212–28.

Map 2. Ceylon: size and communal composition of District population according to the 1953 census.

The area of each circle is proportional to the population of the District which it represents (Districts are named after the District capitals, see Map 1). The area of each sector of a circle is proportional to the population of the community it represents (no attempt has been made to subdivide the small circle for Vavuniya District, where population is 5 per cent Low-Country Sinhalese, 11 per cent Kandyan Sinhalese, 67 per cent Tamil, 8 per cent Ceylon Moor and 7 per cent Indian and Pakistani).

The result is, too, that some 10 per cent of Ceylon's population are in effect without civic status, and are virtually stateless, since Indian citizenship law is itself highly selective.

The Indian Tamils have not unnaturally resented the treatment which they have received; economic necessity keeps them at their jobs, but does not prevent them from striking (see also below, p. 69). The Indian Government has expressed concern on a number of occasions about the status of Indians in Ceylon, and there have been a number of inconclusive rounds of negotiation.

Indian Tamils and other Indians and Pakistanis in Ceylon have also been under attack in other ways. Land legislation has been such that Crown Land cannot be alienated to Indians for agricultural purposes, and there has been pressure for legislation to prevent the alienation to them of Crown Land for other purposes, and of private land for any purpose. The Land Commission of 1955–58 came down heavily, however, against legislation of this sort.[3] Kandyans have also from time to time brought pressure to bear on the Government to acquire estates and to alienate them in small blocks to peasants, and a number of estates have in fact suffered this fate: one effect, clearly, is to replace Indian Tamil wage labour with Sinhalese peasant labour.

But, trouble though there was over the Indian Tamil question during the days of U.N.P. rule, there was no disturbance of the peace; and relations between the Sinhalese and Ceylon Tamils seemed quiet and untroubled, though there were occasional tales of discrimination.

The U.N.P. won the general elections of 1952 easily and it was confidently predicted in Colombo that they would repeat the performance, though perhaps with a reduced majority, in April 1956. But in the event the U.N.P. retained only eight seats compared with the fifty-one to the credit of Bandaranaike's 'Mahajana Eksath Peramuna'

[3] *Interim Report of the Land Commission*, Ceylon Sessional Paper No. 15 of 1957, pp. 33–37.

('People's United Front'). And, as is well known, the ensuing years were darkened by increasing communal tension and disorder, to say nothing of political assassination. In point of fact, communal factors had a great deal to do with Bandaranaike's success, though other considerations also told in his favour. For instance, the turnover in votes was far less marked than the turnover in seats, so that Bandaranaike's victory was not as complete as might appear. Secondly, he had succeeded in engineering a coalition of highly disparate elements, including Trotskyites and others as well as the Sri Lanka Freedom Party, the successor to his old 'Sinhala Maha Sabha' (the fact that the party name is half English and half Sinhalese is highly though unintentionally symbolic); and in arranging a pact with other non-U.N.P. groups under the terms of which the contracting parties agreed not to fight each other where there was a U.N.P. man to be ousted. Again, D. S. Senanayake's tragic death as a result of an accident had robbed his party of his leadership and of his prestige in the country and led to undignified squabbles over the succession. And finally, the U.N.P. as a whole had become lethargic after so long a period in power and, some said, corrupt too.

Bandaranaike was an astute politician, in many ways a typical member of the English-speaking élite, yet with good links with the Sinhalese villages. He was able to nail to his election platform a number of planks varying from 'Up with the Left' and 'Nationalise Foreign Estates' to 'Down with the U.N.P.'. No matter if some of the planks bore mutually contradictory injunctions: each was designed to catch votes somewhere. But Bandaranaike's largest and most useful plank was that which, in effect, repeated the age-old cry 'Religion, Language, Nation'. That this was so potent a vote-catcher in Sinhalese rural areas (where it had its main appeal) was due to a social movement, a sort of second wave of nationalism that had for some time been gathering momentum in the countryside, unsuspected by many in the towns. This was compounded partly of resurgent Buddhism—the tide discerned in the last Chapter brought to full flood by the incidence of *Buddha Jayanti*, the 2,500th anniversary of the Buddha's attainment of nirvana, and fed by hostility to the West and to the U.N.P. (declared to be its agents) as the destroyers of traditional moral, religious and cultural values. Partly, too, the movement in question gained force from a resurgence of traditional Sinhalese culture and, through the literature of former times, of traditional attitudes; most important of all, there was a great move to make Sinhalese the language of the newly independent nation—not English, the language of imperialism, nor Tamil, the language of the traditional enemy.

The M.E.P. were able to pose as the champions of this cause before the U.N.P. changed its policy to favour 'Sinhalese only'. We have already seen the special significance of their language to the Sinhalese, a majority in Ceylon but a minority in a wider context. The language agitation, which was growing strong and even violent by the time of the 1956 elections, was reinforced by economic considerations. For there was, and is, a group in the Sinhalese villages who are of great influence—but have no exact parallel in the West, so that they have been described (incorrectly) as 'Leftists' or 'nationalists'—or, alternatively, ignored. This group consists of such people as Buddhist priests, village shopkeepers, moneylenders and petty landowners, vernacular schoolmasters, and indigenous ('ayurvedic') physicians. They may be called the 'new village leaders' and they have this in common—that they are all intelligent men who have for one reason or another been denied the education in English which had, with some justification, come to be regarded as a passport to a secure and relatively lucrative job, preferably in (Ceylon's principal industry) government service. Their sense of economic frustration has grown in recent years because of what is, in effect, the 'passing of the frontier' in Ceylon terms. For, with the establishment of the plantations, the absorption of waste land in peasant commercial crops, and the growth of population, there is now virtually no usable but uncultivated land left in the lowland Wet Zone or in the hills. The amount of cultivable land *per capita* has been diminishing; the number of rootless, landless labourers and the amount of underemployment and of actual unemployment has been growing. Unemployment has been reinforced by the tendency (not unknown in the West) for those with some education to wish to leave agriculture. But where can they turn, in the absence of industries to absorb them and of a knowledge of English to help them? So the 'educated youth' of Ceylon have become a special category and have swollen the ranks of the discontented.

This complicated discontent—religious, linguistic and economic—has been directed against the élite (who have the coveted jobs and who are alleged to be hostile to true Sinhalese culture and to Buddhism), against the U.N.P. (as the party of the élite) and against the Tamils (who are alleged to hold a highly disproportionate number of jobs and, clearly, are vulnerable in any case at a time of the revival of a backward-looking nationalism). Some hold that this flavour of nationalism has been made all the stronger because the closing of one frontier has coincided with the opening of another, in the lowland Dry Zone and, in particular, in Raja Rata. D. S. Senanayake, for example, was an enthusiastic advocate of a policy of the recolonisation of the Dry Zone and, especially since the conquest of malaria by D.D.T., settlement has gone on at an accelerated rate.[4] It may well be that the feeling that they were restoring ancient glories has done something to quicken a sense of national identity and of historic destiny among the Sinhalese; certainly it has to some extent taken Sinhalese into traditionally Tamil areas and Tamils into traditionally Sinhalese areas, thus increasing the chance of communal disharmony and of serious trouble at times when communal

[4] See B. H. Farmer, *Peasant Colonization in Ceylon*.

feeling has been running high nationally. This is particularly true of the labour force brought in for land development work.

The point must also be made that the factors just passed in review have worked together, each tending to amplify some of the others. For example, the revival of Buddhism has for historical reasons quickened the Sinhalese sense of national identity and helped to precipitate the language issue. And, finally, there has been an element of opportunism at two distinct levels. At the local level, it seems quite clear that the new village leaders have exploited language, religious and communal issues in order to gain power in the village and, in particular, in opposition to that of the older power, traditional village leaders whom the British used as headmen. At the national level, it is also all too clear that Bandaranaike and his group, having sensed what was afoot in the villages and having determined to exploit the issues involved in order to gain power, inevitably exaggerated all the feelings and tensions that were so intertwined in the village situation. In part, no doubt, this was unintentional; but there is evidence too that feeling, especially on communal issues, was deliberately whipped up for political ends. Bandaranaike has received many labels in the West—nationalist, socialist, Buddhist revivalist. He may have been all of these things, but above all he was an opportunist. He did, however, appeal to the common man and persuade him that the Government was his Government; and since his death a great legend has grown up about him that has served his party well and that has been assiduously exploited.

Very soon after coming into power in April 1956 the Bandaranaike Government pressed ahead with legislation to make Sinhalese the sole national language, and this led directly to a reaction from the Ceylon Tamils, who saw the legislation and the emotions behind it as a threat not only to their culture and their identity but to their means of earning a living. There was rioting in Colombo when

Ceylon Tamil leaders sought to perform *satyagraha* (passive civil disobedience) in protest, and even uglier riots in the Gal Oya valley, an area of recent colonisation in the eastern Dry Zone lowland with a mixed population and, moreover, a large foot-loose labour force.

Over 150 people died in the 1956 riots. In 1957 the Tamil leaders threatened *satyagraha* again, and the upshot was a pact between Bandaranaike and S. J. V. Chelvanayakam, the leader of the Tamil Federalists, which was supposed to permit the 'reasonable use of Tamil' in the northern and eastern Provinces; but communal incidents persisted.

The Tamil Federal Party had meanwhile emerged as the strongest political party in Jaffna and other Ceylon Tamil areas. In earlier years there had been other Tamil parties, and non-communal parties had made some headway. But the immediate reaction to the threat of resurgent Sinhalese nationalism was to strengthen the hand of the most extreme Tamil party, the Federalists, who sought a federal structure for Ceylon with local autonomy for the Tamil areas. Another Tamil reaction was a tendency for Ceylon Tamils living in isolated groups in Sinhalese areas to retreat to Jaffna; many swore that they would live in simple poverty as peasants, as their fathers had, rather than run the risk of assault or even death in the Sinhalese areas.

Then in April 1958 Mr. Bandaranaike, under pressure from a group of militant Buddhist priests, abrogated the pact that he had made with Chelvanayakam—and swung Tamil opinion even more firmly behind the Federalists. But, he protested, he would nevertheless introduce legislation to guarantee 'fair play for the Tamils'—and was greeted with protests, louder than ever, from Sinhalese communalists, who began to shout 'Ceylon for the Sinhalese'. Incident followed incident all over the island, and it seems quite clear that politicians were at work adding fuel to the communal fires, if not directly encouraging acts of violence. By 24 May there were 'carefully calculated rumours' in Polonnaruwa that there was to be a Tamil invasion from Trincomalee and Batticaloa, and rioting became extremely ugly: Tamils were beaten up and their women were raped, not by colonists in the large local colonisation scheme, but by members of the foot-loose labour force of the sort which two years earlier had caused so much trouble in Gal Oya.[5] The rioting grew from bad to worse, and many Tamils were murdered. The Government handled the situation badly, and rioting spread to other parts of the island. In many places it was directed not only against Tamils but against government officers who were trying to preserve order. Not surprisingly, there was some retaliation by Tamil thugs in Batticaloa, Jaffna and elsewhere against isolated Sinhalese. Eventually, to cut a long, terrible and disgraceful story short, a State of Emergency was declared, and slowly order was restored: for this great credit is due to the Governor-General, Sir Oliver Goonetilleke, who virtually took the government of the country into his own hands.

With order restored, the Government faced violent criticism all over the country for 'using the army to help the Tamils' and for killing Sinhalese to do so; and a scapegoat was sought. It is said that at a meeting of the Government Parliamentary Group demands were made for the arrest of Chelvanayakam and other Federalist leaders on the grounds that they had plotted against the Government; certainly on 4 June 1958, with the Emergency in its second week and life returning to normal, the Federal leaders were arrested, with many members of their party; a week later a single member of an extreme Sinhalese organisation, K. M. P. Rajaratne, was placed under house arrest.

Since those saddening days of 1958 Ceylon has had its share of trouble: political assassination, wave upon wave of strikes, economic crisis after economic crisis, and an attempted military *coup*. But so far at any rate the terror of communal rioting has not returned. In March 1961,

[5] A full and highly credible account of the 1958 riots is given in Tarzie Vittachi, *Emergency '58* (London, André Deutsch, 1958).

however, Tamils in Jaffna and elsewhere once again organised *satyagraha* as a reaction to a further phase in the Sinhalese-only language policy, and for a time there was even a separate Tamil-organised postal service. Once again there was a State of Emergency, the establishment of what amounted to military rule in Jaffna, and the detention of prominent Tamils. The Government (by now headed by Mrs. Bandaranaike, S. W. R. D. Bandaranaike's widow) seemed at times near to panic, perhaps from fear of a recurrence of 1958, perhaps from fear of joint action between Ceylon and Indian Tamils in Ceylon, perhaps because the activity of the 'Dravida Munnethra Kazagam' (D.M.K.) and other Tamil nationalist parties in south India at the time appeared to heighten the risk of an even wider coalition of Tamils and to quicken once again Sinhalese fears of being a minority in south India as a whole.

The D.M.K. has, in fact, been working among Indian Tamils in Up-Country Ceylon, and in July 1962 was proscribed by the Ceylon Government. This drew the fire of Chelvanayakam, who described as 'undemocratic' the banning of an organisation 'engaged in peaceable political activity' and 'working for the liberation of the Up-Country Tamils politically and economically'.[6] Mrs. Bandaranaike only a few weeks later warned the Federal Party itself against campaigning in the planting areas, and is stated to have drawn the report from a Tamil Federalist spokesman that it was 'a fundamental principle of our party to forge unity among Tamil-speaking people'.[7] It is thus always possible that Sinhalese chauvinism will succeed where everything else has failed and provoke the breaking-down of the isolation of the Indian Tamils in Ceylon, with results that none can foretell.

The communal situation in Ceylon thus remains delicate. Many Tamils have left the service of the Government, some

[6] *Ceylon News*, 2 August 1962.
[7] As report in *Ceylon News Letter*, 20 September 1962 (this is a Government hand-out).

have left the country. It is reported that some Ceylon Tamil *harijans* have found their own solution, the characteristic solution of a group that has nothing to lose in traditional society, by becoming Buddhists.[8] Small minorities, on the whole, appear to be trying to come to terms with Sinhalese nationalism: some Moors, for example, seem to be forsaking Tamil speech for Sinhalese, and the Burgher community is treading very cautiously. 'Second-wave' Sinhalese nationalism is, naturally, so closely tied up with Buddhism of a militant kind (if this does not appear a contradiction in terms) that the Christians, and in particular the Roman Catholics, have found themselves under attack; in fact, the state has taken over almost all denominational schools. Some Karāva Catholics have felt that it is really Sinhalese Goyigama Buddhism that is attacking them, so that they are doubly vulnerable, both as a caste minority that has had its trouble with the Goyigama (see pp. 49–50 above) and as Roman Catholics. But the intricate relation of caste to the present political scene in Ceylon is too complicated to be examined here, even if adequate evidence were available.[9] The upper middle-class élite, too, feels itself under attack, given the quality of the social movement in the country which is the spearhead of the modern Sinhalese nationalist movement. Certainly it is very difficult to see what its future is, and one fears for the morale and for the future of the essential organs of government and of society that depend so heavily on it: the Civil Service and indeed the public service generally, the University, the Planning Commission, to mention only a few.

The truth, unpalatable though it may be to some, is simply that no group, no body unacceptable to the present second wave of resurgent, Sinhalese Buddhist nationalism has any chance of constitutional power in contemporary Ceylon. The failure of the parties of the Left to make

[8] *Ceylon News*, 15 November 1961.
[9] This theme is explored in a tentative way in B. H. Farmer, 'The Social Basis of Nationalism in Ceylon ', *St. Antony's Papers* (in the Press).

headway in the last two elections (in April and July 1960), for example, is not really due, outside the towns, to the resolution of issues along Left versus Right lines, as was so persistently reported in the British Press; it was simply that the two principal parties concerned had stood for a non-communal policy and, in fact, for parity on the language issue. Similarly, whatever Dudley Senanayake and the wiser among the present leaders of the revived U.N.P. may privately feel about the need for national unity, they cannot hope for electoral success in rural Sinhalese areas unless they appear to stand for Buddhism, and for Sinhalese-only. The U.N.P., in fact, opposed the Bandaranaike–Chelvanayakam pact, largely on the grounds that it would have prevented colonisation by Sinhalese in Tamil areas. Christians in the Cabinet, like Felix Dias Bandaranaike, have to prove themselves more Buddhist than the Buddhists. And meanwhile members of minorities, whether caste, communal or religious minorities, feel insecure. There is always the possibility that worsening economic conditions may bring the temperature to the boil again—of its own accord or because politicians feel the need to divert attention from the plight of the poor of all kinds.

Ceylon is indeed a divided nation. The reader may be inclined to form the conclusion that it was always so, and that optimistic views on national unity held in Ceylon at the coming of independence, and repeated by commentators in other parts of the world, rested on illusion or ignorance. Certainly, given the historical traditions of the Sinhalese and their particular national complexes, and given the history which set down in their midst the particular minorities that have come to exist in Ceylon, trouble might have been foreseen. But need it have been as violent as in fact it was? Constitutional safeguards might conceivably have done something to control the violence of the communal dispute; though, since the Senanayake Government found a way of disenfranchising the Indian Tamils, one is left to wonder what value other safeguards might have had in the event and in the Ceylon setting. Perhaps one of Ceylon's greatest misfortunes, given hindsight wisdom, is that its first wave of nationalism, if it can be called such, was so exclusively an affair of the élite, pleasant negotiators though British statesmen found them; and that the second wave of nationalism should have proceeded separately, fighting the élite and its values instead of being guided and controlled by them. Here Ceylon, possibly, was less fortunate than India, where the alliance symbolised and cemented by the relation between Nehru and Gandhi contrived to subsume in one powerful movement both traditional and forward-looking nationalism. But if there is a moral here, it is too late for Ceylon to profit from it: perhaps if D. S. Senanayake had lived he might have been more able than his successors to see what was needed. But, maybe, it is not too late for the lesson to be learnt elsewhere.

SELECT BIBLIOGRAPHY

Sydney D. Bailey, *Ceylon* (London, Hutchinson's University Library, 1952).

Ceylon: Report of the Special Commission on the Constitution (Donoughmore Report) (London, H.M.S.O., Cmd. 3131, 1928).

Ceylon: Report of the Special Commission on Constitutional Reform (Soulbury Report) (London, H.M.S.O., Cmd. 6677, 1945).

H. W. Codrington, *A Short History of Ceylon* (London, Macmillan, 1939).

Colvin R. De Silva, *Ceylon under the British Occupation, 1795–1833* 2 vols. (Colombo, Colombo Apothecaries, 1953).

B. H. Farmer, 'Ceylon' in O. H. K. Spate, *India and Pakistan*, 2nd. ed. (London, Methuen and New York, Dutton, 1957).

B. H. Farmer, *Pioneer Peasant Colonization in Ceylon* (London, Oxford University Press for the Royal Institute of International Affairs, 1957).

B. H. Farmer, 'Politics in Ceylon'. in Saul Rose (editor), *The Political Evolution of Southern Asia since Independence* (London, Macmillan, 1963).

B. H. Farmer, 'The Social Basis of Nationalism in Ceylon', *St. Antony's Papers* (in the press).

Sir W. Ivor Jennings, *Nationalism and Political Development in Ceylon*, (New York, Institute of Pacific Relations, 1950).

Sir W. Ivor Jennings, *The Constitution of Ceylon*, 2nd. ed. (Bombay, Oxford University Press, 1951).

Kandyan Peasantry Commission, Report of the, Ceylon Sessional Paper No. 18 of 1951 (Colombo, Government Press, 1951).

E. R. Leach, (editor), *Aspects of Caste in South India, Ceylon and North-West Pakistan*, Cambridge Papers in Social Anthropology No. 2 (Cambridge, Cambridge University Press for the Department of Archaeology and Anthropology, 1960).

E. F. C. Ludowyk, *The Story of Ceylon* (London, Faber, 1962).

SELECT BIBLIOGRAPHY

G. C. Mendis, *The Early History of Ceylon*, 3rd. ed. (Calcutta, Y.M.C.A. Publishing House, 1938).

G. C. Mendis, *Ceylon under the British*, 2nd. ed. (Colombo, Colombo Apothecaries, 1948).

G. C. Mendis, *Ceylon Today and Yesterday* (Colombo, Associated Newspapers, 1957).

S. Namasivayan, *The Legislature of Ceylon, 1928–1948* (London, Faber for Nuffield College, 1951).

S. Paranavitana (editor), *University of Ceylon History of Ceylon*, vol. 1, Parts I and II (Colombo, Ceylon University Press, 1959 and 1960).

L. H. Horace Perera, *Additional Chapters to H. W. Codrington's 'A Short History of Ceylon* (London, Macmillan, 1952).

P. E. Pieris, *Ceylon and the Hollanders, 1658–1798*, 3rd. ed. (Colombo, Colombo Apothecaries, n.d.)

Bryce Ryan, *Caste in Modern Ceylon* (New Brunswick, Rutgers University Press, 1953).

A. J. Tresidder, *Ceylon* (Princeton, Van Nostrand, 1960).

Tarzie Vittachi, *Emergency '58* (London, André Deutsch, 1958).

Tarzie Vittachi, *The Brown Sahib* (London, André Deutsch, 1962).

I. D. S. Weerawardena, *Ceylon General Election 1956* (Colombo, Gunasena, 1960).

W. Howard Wriggins, *Ceylon: Dilemmas of a New Nation* (Princeton, Princeton University Press, 1960).